12.50

Essay Index

DATE DUE	
AUG - 8 1994	
SEP 2 4 2002	
OCT 0 9 2002	
NOV 2 8 2002	
DEC 1 9 2002	

DEMCO, INC. 38-2931

Backgrounds of Literature

Dove Cottage, Grasmere

Backgrounds of Literature

By

Hamilton Wright Mabie

NEW EDITION

Illustrated

Essay Index Reprint Series

Essay Index

BOOKS FOR LIBRARIES PRESS
FREEPORT, NEW YORK

New Edition First Published 1904
Reprinted 1970

STANDARD BOOK NUMBER:
8369-1617-4

LIBRARY OF CONGRESS CATALOG CARD NUMBER:
72-111846

PRINTED IN THE UNITED STATES OF AMERICA

CONTENTS

LIST OF ILLUSTRATIONS

x LIST OF ILLUSTRATIONS

THE LAKE COUNTRY
AND WORDSWORTH

THE LAKE COUNTRY
AND WORDSWORTH

He spoke, and loosed our hearts in tears.
He laid us as we lay at birth,
On the cool flowery lap of earth;
Smiles broke from us and we had ease;
The hills were round us, and the breeze
Went o'er the sunlit fields again;
Our foreheads felt the wind and rain.
Our youth return'd; for there was shed
On spirits that had long been dead,
Spirits dried up and closely furl'd,
The freshness of the early world.

O wrote Matthew Arnold in 1850, when the long life of Wordsworth ended and he was laid at rest in the churchyard at Grasmere, the Rotha sweeping past his grave with the freshness and purity of the mountains in its bosom.

3

THE LAKE COUNTRY

Half a century has passed since the bells in the old square tower tolled on that memorable day, but the peace with which the poet touched the fevered life of the century has not lost its healing, nor has his message lost its power. There are still differences of opinion concerning minor points in his work, but his genius is no longer questioned; and his art, in its best moments, has won complete recognition. Some foreign critics, it is true, have doubted and even sneered; but one of the most valuable of recent contributions to the large literature which has grown up about Wordsworth comes from the hand of a very intelligent and sympathetic French critic. It is safe to say that, in the settled opinion of this country and of England, Wordsworth gave the world between 1798 and 1815 work that has enriched English poetry for all time both in substance and in form. For this poetry had not only a new music for the ear which made men think suddenly of mountain brooks; it had also a new view of nature and a new conception of life.

A poet so freighted with spiritual insight, with meditative habit, and with moral fervor, is

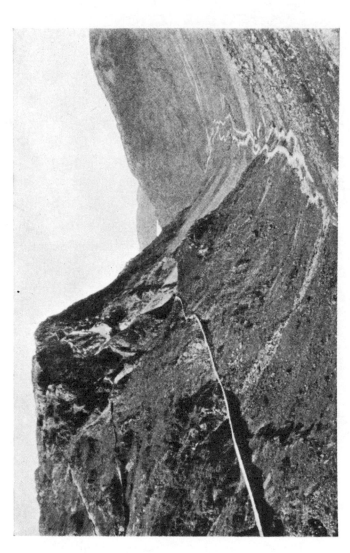

Honister Crag and Pass

always in danger of straining his art and dissipating its magic in the endeavor to produce ethical results; and a touch of didacticism banishes the bloom and dissolves the spell. There was in Wordsworth a natural stiffness of mind which showed itself more distinctly as time impaired the vivacity of his moods and the freshness of his imagination. He was, by instinct and the habit of a lifetime, a moralist; and there were times when he came perilously near being a preacher in verse. He was, as often happens, radically unlike the popular impression of him; he and Keats have been widely and astonishingly misunderstood. One constantly comes upon expressions of the feeling that Wordsworth had the calmness of the philosophic temper, and that he was by nature self-poised and cold; and this in the face of the fact that one of the great qualities of his verse is its passion! Wordsworth was, by nature, headstrong, ardent, passionate, with great capacity for emotion and suffering; the sorrows of his life shook him as an oak is shaken by a tempest, and years afterward, when he referred to the deaths of his children or of his brother, his emotion was painful to look upon. He bore himself with a noble fortitude through the trials and disappointments of his long career; but that fortitude was won through struggle. He had a stubborn will, which became inflexible when a principle was involved; he passed through a great spiritual crisis when the French Revolution first liberated and then blasted the hopes of ardent and generous spirits in Europe; he sought seclusion and maintained it to the end; he was rejected and derided by the great majority of those who made literary opinion during his youth and maturity; and his verse brought him no returns, although he had both the need and the wholesome desire for adequate payment for honorable work.

All these and other conditions told against the free development of the pure poetic quality in Wordsworth's nature, and against that spontaneity which is the source of natural magic in poetry. It is not surprising that he wrote so much didactic verse; it is surprising that he wrote so much poetry of surpassing charm and beauty. When all deductions are made from his work, there remains a body of poetry large enough and beautiful enough to place the poet among the greatest of English singers. At his best no one has more of that magic which lends to thought the enchantment of a melody that seems to flow out of its heart as the brook runs shining and singing out of the heart of the hills. No English poet has command of a purer music, and none has more to say to the spirit; he speaks to the ear, to the imagination, to the intellect, and to the soul of his fellows. He was always high-minded, devoted to his work, stainless in all his relations; during fifteen golden years he was so in tune with Nature that she breathed through him as the wind breathes through the harp, and the deep silence of the hills became a haunting music in his verse, and the inarticulate murmur of the mountain streams a reconciling and restful melody to tired spirits and sorrow-smitten hearts. Such a life is a spiritual achievement; add to it a noble body of poetry, and the measure of Wordsworth's greatness and service becomes more clear, although that measure has not yet been finally taken.

In this poetry Nature is not only presented

9

in every aspect, but is interpreted in a way which was in effect a revelation. It is true, poets as far back as Lucretius had conceived of Nature as a whole, and had felt and expressed the inspiration which flowed from this great conception; but Wordsworth was the first poet in whose imagination this view of the world was completely mastered and assimilated; the first poet who adequately presented Nature, not only as a vast unity of form and life, but as a sublime symbol; the first poet who succeeded in blending the life of man with Nature with such spiritual insight that the deeper correspondences between the two were brought into clear view, and their subtle and secret relations indicated. He is constantly spoken of as preeminently the poet of Nature, because in no other English verse does Nature fill so vast a place as in his poetry; but he was even more distinctly the poet of the spirit of man, discerning everywhere in Nature those spiritual forces and verities which came to consciousness in his own soul, and those hints and suggestions of spiritual truth which found in his own spirit an interpreter.

Hawkshead, where Wordsworth went to School

AND WORDSWORTH

It was inevitable that a poetry of Nature which was, at bottom, a poetry of life, with Nature as a background, a symbol, a spiritual energy, a living environment, should have its roots deep in the soil and should reflect, not general impressions of a universe, but aspects, glimpses, views of a world close at hand. In art great conceptions are successfully presented only when they find forms so beautiful and inevitable that the thought seems born in the form as the soul is lodged in the body; not conditioned by it, but so much a part of it that it cannot be localized, and so pervasive that it irradiates and spiritualizes every part. In like manner, in his best moments, Wordsworth fills our vision with the beauty of some actual scene or place before he opens the imagination by natural and inevitable dilation to some great poetic idea. In the noble " Lines written above Tintern Abbey," in which his imagination rises to a great height and his diction rises with it on even wing, we are first made to see with marvelous distinctness the steep and lonely cliffs, the dark sycamore, the orchard-tufts, the hedge-rows—" little lines of sportive wood run

13

wild "—the pastoral farms and wreaths of smoke, before we are brought under the spell of

> That serene and blessed mood,
> In which the affections lead us on,

and we become living souls and see into the heart of things. In like manner the great Ode rises from familiar things—the rose, the moon, the birds, the lamb, the sweet, homely sights and sounds—to that sublime height from which the whole sweep and range of life become visible. And the lover of Wordsworth who recalls the Highland girl, the dancing daffodils, and a hundred other imperishable figures and scenes, knows with what unerring instinct the poet fastens upon the familiar and near when he purposes to flash into the imagination the highest truths.

Wordsworth's poetry has a singular unity and consistency; from beginning to end it is bound together not only by great ideas which continually reappear, but it is harmonized by a background which remains unchanged from stage to stage. This double unity was made possible by the good fortune of a lifelong residence in the Lake Country. With the exception of the years at Cambridge, when he was a student in St. John's College, and later in London and Dorsetshire, and of occasional visits to the Continent, the poet spent his whole life almost within sight of Skiddaw and Helvellyn. In childhood, youth, maturity, and age he saw the same noble masses of mountain, the same sleeping or moving surfaces of water; he heard the same music of running streams and the same deep harmonies of tempests among the hills. The sources of his poetry were in his own nature, but its scenery, its incidents, its occasions, are, with few exceptions, to be found in the Lake Country. No one can catch all the tones of his verse who has not heard the rush of wind and the notes of hidden streams in that beautiful region; no one can fully possess the rich and splendid atmosphere which gathers about his greater passages who has not seen the unsearchable glory of the sunset when the upper Vales are filled with a mist which is transformed into such effulgence of light as never yet came "within the empire of any earthly pencil." In a word, the poetry of Wordsworth is rooted

15

in the Lake Country as truly as the other
flora of that region; and the spirit and quality
of the landscape not only come to the surface
in separate poems and in detached lines, but
penetrate and irradiate the whole body of his
verse.

THE poet was born at Cockermouth, on the 7th
of April, 1770, the second son of John Wordsworth, law agent of the Earl of Lonsdale. The
town is in the northeastern part of the Lake
region, not many miles from the English Chan-
nel, and within sound of the water of the Derwent. On the main street of the old market
town stands the plain, substantial, two-storied
house, spacious and comfortable, in which William and Dorothy were born; for the two names
ought never to be separated, the sister's passionate devotion and genius contributing not
only to the brother's growth and comfort, but
to his work. To the south rises the castle, half
in ruins; about are soft, grassy hills. The
garden at the back of the house, with its hedges
and the river murmuring near, was the play-
ground of the children. There flowers bloomed

Kirkstone Pass

and birds built safely, and the days went by in
a deep and beautiful calm:

> Stay near me: do not take thy flight!
> A little longer stay in sight!
> Much converse do I find in thee,
> Historian of my infancy!
> Float near me: do not yet depart.
> Dead times revive in thee:
> Thou bring'st, gay creature as thou art!
> A solemn image to my heart,
>   My father's family!

> Oh! pleasant, pleasant were the days,
> The time, when, in our childish plays,
> My sister Emmeline and I
> Together chased the butterfly!
> A very hunter did I rush
> Upon the prey; with leaps and springs
> I followed on from brook to bush;
> But she, God love her! feared to brush
>   The dust from off its wings.

In the " Prelude " Wordsworth has left to
the world a unique autobiography; a human
document of the highest interest. In this story
of his poetic life the landscape of his physical
life is reflected in almost numberless glimpses,
from his childhood to those rich years at Gras-

mere. In this meditative, descriptive poem, as in a quiet stream, his childhood and youth are preserved, and we are enabled to note the scenes and incidents which left their permanent impress on his memory. Under the northwest tower of the Castle at Cockermouth the Derwent runs swift and deep, and sweeps tumultuously over the blue-gray gravel of the shallows which spread out from the bank opposite. The boy never forgot this striking effect, and years after he wrote of

> . . . the shadow of those towers
> That yet survive, a shattered monument
> Of feudal sway, the bright blue river passed
> Along the margin of our terrace walk.

Standing in the garden at the back of the house, he saw constantly the footpath that led from the ford over the rocky brow of a neighboring hill; and that worn line of human travel became a highway to his imagination:

> . . . a disappearing line,
> One daily present to my eyes, that crossed
> The naked summit of a far-off hill
> Beyond the limits that my feet had trod,
> Was like an invitation into space
> Boundless, or guide into eternity.

In 1778 the boy was sent to the Grammar School at Hawkshead, founded by Archbishop Sandys in 1585, at that memorable time when William Shakespeare, escaping from the tasks of the Stratford Grammar School and the quiet which broods along the banks of the slow-moving Avon, had gone up to London to seek and find the greatest fortune of literary opportunity and fame which has yet come in the way of mortal man. The school is still largely unchanged; there is a spacious room on the ground floor where the ancient hum of industrious boys is still heard; there is a small library made up of gifts from the students, each pupil presenting a volume when he leaves the school. The names of the Masters are preserved on a tablet in this room, and in an oaken chest the original charter of the school is kept. The old oak benches in the lower room bear witness to the traditional activity of the jack-knife, and " W. Wordsworth " is cut deeply in the wood. Here the boy worked at his books for eight happy years; boarding, as was the custom of the place, with a village dame—Anne Tyson—for whom he came to have a deep and lasting affection. The

21

house in which she lived, like its fellows in the village, is small and unpretentious. The village lies in the beautiful country between Windermere and Coniston Water, with Esthwaite Water close at hand. It is a quaint old market town, with narrow streets, low archways, houses with many-paned windows; the old church dominating the place:

> The snow-white church upon the hill
> Sits like a thronèd lady, sending out
> A gracious look all over her domain.

The " Prelude " lingers long over the scenes, incidents, and experiences of the eight years at Hawkshead; and it would be quite impossible to find a locality more nobly planned for the unfolding and enrichment of a poet's imagination. The lover of Wordsworth can still feel something of the spell which was laid upon the boy in those golden days of fresh and aspiring youth. The teaching which the school gave was, for its time, admirable; but the deepest education was gained out of school hours, and, largely, out of doors. The memory of those years was always fresh and grateful:

Ullswater

AND WORDSWORTH

Well do I call to mind the very week
When I was first intrusted to the care
Of that sweet Valley.

The " Prelude " makes us aware of the spiritual richness and growth of these school days; of the joy of reading and the deeper joy of seeing; of long walks of exploration; of silent hours upon Esthwaite, or, in vacation, upon Windermere, when the deep and solemn beauty of mountain and star sank into his heart:

Dear native Regions, wheresoe'er shall close
My mortal course, there will I think on you;
Dying, will cast on you a backward look;
Even as this setting sun (albeit the Vale
Is nowhere touched by one memorial gleam)
Doth with the fond remains of his last power
Still linger, and a farewell luster sheds
On the dear mountain-tops where first he rose.

Within easy walking distance one comes upon some of the most impressive or enchanting scenery of the Lake Country. Windermere, with its group of mountains; the striking lines of the Langdale Pikes, and other peaks, crowd the horizon in all directions. To the west, over the hill, through lovely stretches of meadow or across the moorland, lies Coniston Water, with the massive front of Coniston Old Man rising across the quiet lake. One cannot look down on that exquisite Valley without thinking of Brantwood, and of the last of the group of great writers who were contemporaneous with Wordsworth's later years.

The leisure hours of that happy time were not, however, wholly given over to wandering and solitude; there was companionship with books as well:

Of my earliest days at school [writes the poet] I have little to say, but that they were very happy ones, chiefly because I was left at liberty there, and in the vacations, to read whatever books I liked. For example, I read all Fielding's works, Don Quixote, Gil Blas, and any part of Swift that I liked, Gulliver's Travels and The Tale of a Tub being both much to my taste. It may be, perhaps, as well to mention that the first verses which I wrote were a task imposed by my master—the subject, The Summer Vacation; and of my own accord I added others upon Return to School. There was nothing remarkable in either poem; but I was called upon, among other scholars, to write verses upon the completion of the second centenary from the foundation of the school in 1585 by Archbishop Sandys. These verses were much admired—

far more than they deserved, for they were but a tame imitation of Pope's versification, and a little in his style.

The real education of the boy—the liberation of his imagination and the unfolding of his spiritual nature—was gained, however, in the woods and fields and upon the quiet lakes. Esthwaite, Windermere, and Winander, and the mountains which encircled them and made them a world by themselves, were his most potent teachers. Here, in boyhood, he began to reveal that union of exact observation with imaginative insight which was to give his poetry vividness of pictorial effect and depth of spiritual suggestion. He learned both to see the object upon which his eye rested, and also, by a sudden extension of vision, to discern its significance in that invisible order of which all things seen are but types and symbols. And out of this clarity and range of vision there came the double beauty of his verse: the beauty of the flower or tree or landscape suddenly and vividly presented to the imagination, and the beauty of the great world of earth and sky which enfolds flower and tree and landscape;

the beauty of the daffodil dancing along the margin of the bay, and that other beauty which flashes upon

> . . . that inward eye
> Which is the bliss of solitude.

In October, 1787, Wordsworth left the Lake Country for the first time and took up his residence in the southwestern corner of the first quadrangle of St. John's College, Cambridge. Here he found another kind of beauty: the beauty of low-lying fields, of streams that run through marshes to the sea, of low, veiled skies. Here, too, was the ripe loveliness of an ancient seat of learning; and here, above all, were the richest traditions and associations of English poetry. Those glorious windows and noble roofs which Milton loved so well Wordsworth loved also, and from those dark carven seats where one sits to-day under the spell of choral singing of almost angelic sweetness he doubtless searched, with reverent gaze,

> That branching roof
> Self-poised, and scooped into ten thousand cells
> Where light and shade repose, where music dwells

Rydal Mount

Lingering, and wandering on as loth to die—
Like thoughts whose very sweetness yieldeth proof
That they were born for immortality.

Having taken his Bachelor's degree in January, 1791, Wordsworth went up to London, uncertain as to his future vocation. Every reader of his poetry knows how vividly he saw certain things in London—the thrush that sang on Wood Street, and by the magic of its notes made poor Susan suddenly aware of trees and mountains, of rolling vapor and running streams; and that noble vision from Westminster Bridge; but the great city touched him mainly as it reminded him of things remote from its turmoil and alien to its mighty rush and war of strife and toil. In November of the same year he landed in France, at the very moment when the hopes of humanity were still full winged on their sublimest flight; hopes so soon to fall, maimed and bruised, to the earth whence they had risen with such exultant joy. The spiritual crisis through which the ardent young poet passed lies outside the scope of this article; it may be said in passing, however, that those who are tempted to make the usual commonplace comments on his subsequent change of attitude will do well to study first the temperament of one whose nature had a kind of ocean-like capacity for emotion, and whose convictions were born in absolute integrity of thought. The world would not willingly lose Browning's striking lines on " The Lost Leader "; but the world is glad to remember that the younger poet, with characteristic candor, in later and wiser years disclaimed his interpretation of the older poet's course.

In 1795 Wordsworth made his first home at Racedown, in Dorsetshire. His sister joined him, and that beautiful companionship, which was to be one of the prime sources of his inspiration, brought him calmness and hope after months of darkness and discouragement. Here began that long career which was not only to develop poetic genius of a high order, but to illustrate a devotion to the things of the spirit so nobly sustained that the history of literature hardly affords its parallel. The beginnings were not very promising; the poet seemed to need the touch of some quicker mind than his own. The impulse came two years later when Coleridge became the guest of the quiet household, and in one of the long walks in which the two poets and Dorothy Words-worth found such delight, the "Ancient Mar-iner" was planned. In the autumn of the fol-lowing year a new date was made in English literature by the appearance of the "Lyrical Ballads." To that slender volume Wordsworth contributed both his weakness and his strength; it contained "Goody Blake" and "The Idiot Boy," but it also contained "Expostulation and Reply" and " The Tables Turned." Above all, it gave the world the "Lines written above Tin-tern Abbey," in which the genius of the poet touched its highest reach of insight and power.

The poet was now on the threshold of his great career; there were before him fifteen years in which the breath of inspiration touched him again and again, and he sang with the mag-ical ease of the bird; after this productive dec-ade and a half the glow slowly faded, the spell was broken, the magic lost. At the very begin-ning of this epoch in his spiritual and artistic growth, Wordsworth, with his sister, returned to the Lake Country, from which he never again departed save for brief journeys or visits. In the very heart of that lovely region he found the home of his genius and of his affections. "To be at Grasmere," wrote Dorothy, "is like being at a natural church. To spend one's holiday there is like having a week of Sundays." And now, nearly a century later, the Vale still keeps its ancient silence despite the tide of travel which follows the highways. One may stand to-day in the ancient churchyard and feel the peace of the landscape enfolding him as it enfolded Wordsworth. The latest poet to celebrate the sacred associations of the place has not missed the repose which the older poet loved so well:

> Afar though nation be on nation hurled,
> And life with toil and ancient pain depressed,
> Here one may scarce believe the whole wide world
> Is not at peace; and all men's hearts at rest.

In December, 1799, when the Wordsworths took possession of Dove Cottage, the tiny, blue-gray stone house was almost without neighbors, and the lake lay before it like a mirror; to-day it is part of a small but compactly built village. It faces the lake, which is but a short

Striding Edge, Helvellyn

distance from its door; there is a small orchard and garden at the back, so rich in foliage that it is like a fragrant bower; the spring still overflows in its little bowl; the rocks, overhung with vines, rise abruptly from the natural seat which Coleridge cut for Wordsworth; and the outlines of the house are almost invisible, so rich are the masses of vine and foliage which have overgrown and enriched it. Nature has taken the Cottage into her own keeping and made it part of the landscape. The elder-tree which once hung its blossoms near the little porch has gone, but a profusion of wild flowers obliterates all traces of its loss. Through a tiny vestibule the visitor enters the largest room in the house, and is amazed to find it so small; for the greatness of the poetry with which the Cottage is associated somehow affects the image one has unconsciously made of it. Sixteen feet long and twelve broad, with dark oak wainscoting from floor to ceiling, a large fireplace, lighted by a cottage window embowered in jasmine— this was the place where Wordsworth received his friends, and where, far into the night, Coleridge's magical voice went sounding the deeps of thought. Climbing the narrow stairs, one comes to a tiny room where the poet kept his books and where he often wrote; his study was, however, out-of-doors. In the little guest-rooms Coleridge, Scott, De Quincey slept. In one of these rooms Coleridge first read "Christabel" to Wordsworth; there Dorothy and Coleridge often talked until the stars began to fade. "Every sight and sound reminds me of Coleridge," wrote Dorothy in later years; "dear, dear fellow—of his many talks to us, by day and night—of all dear things." In the house, or about it, gather some of the richest traditions of English literature. That marvelous boy, Hartley Coleridge, played in the garden; the small figure of the "Opium Eater," with his dark, expressive face, was often seen in the same garden which, years later, was to be the silent witness of his own strange struggles; within the shelter of this orchard-garden, too, Southey read aloud "Thalaba"; here Sir Humphry Davy brought not only his fame but his unfailing charm of gracious manners and gayety of spirits; and here the Magician of the North wove those ancient spells which none who came near enough to understand his noble nature ever escaped. On a memorable day in 1805, Davy, Scott, and Wordsworth climbed the long and rugged ascent of Helvellyn—

> Old Helvellyn's brow,
> Where once together, in his days of strength,
> We stood rejoicing as if earth were free
> From sorrow, like the sky above our heads.

No presence, however great, lends such beauty and dignity to Dove Cottage as Dorothy Wordsworth gave it out of the richness and nobility of her rare nature. Here she showed, as in a parable, the imperishable sweetness of self-forgetful love; here, in lifelong devotion, she poured out the treasures of her mind and heart for the enrichment of one who, without the warmth of affection, the quick sympathy, the fruitful suggestiveness she gave him, would have been poor indeed, with all his later fame:

> The blessing of my later years
> Was with me when I was a boy;
> She gave me eyes, she gave me ears,
> And humble cares, and delicate fears,
> A heart, the fountain of sweet tears,
> And love, and joy, and thought.

THE LAKE COUNTRY

To this cottage came, later, the wife who was to widen without impairing the circle of comprehension and devotion which wove about the poet a magical barrier against the coldness of the world. No man of genius ever owed more to women than Wordsworth, and none has more richly repaid their devotion; for none has interpreted the finest qualities of womanhood with greater purity of insight. The most magnificent compliment ever paid to a woman was penned by Shakespeare, whose genius is never more searching in its insight or felicitous in phrase than when it deals with ideal women; but Wordsworth's tributes to the highest qualities of womanhood are unsurpassed in delicacy and dignity. Who has ever spoken of woman with a finer instinct than the poet who wrote:

> And she hath smiles to earth unknown;
> Smiles, that with motion of their own
> Do spread, and sink, and rise;
> That come and go with endless play,
> And ever, as they pass away,
> Are hidden in her eyes.

But Dove Cottage was but a personal shelter in a country which, in its entirety, was the home

Langdale Pikes

of Wordsworth's genius. " This is the place where he keeps his books," said a servant to the visitor at Rydal Mount; "his study is out-of-doors." From 1798 to the hour of his death in 1850 the poet lived in the larger world which spread from his door to the horizon. He knew every path, summit, glen, ravine, outlook in that country; he was on intimate terms with every flower, tree, bird; he saw the most deli-cate and elusive play of expression on the face of that world, the shy motions of its most fugi-tive life; he heard every sound which issued from it. One has to walk but a little way from the cottage to see, spread before him, the ma-jesty and loveliness of that landscape. The old road from Grasmere to Ambleside, which Wordsworth haunted not only with his pres-ence but with the murmured tones of his verse, climbs the near hill, and there lies the vaster world!—the little blue-gray village of Gras-mere, at the head of the lake on the right, with the great mass of Helvellyn towering behind it; stretches of green meadows fringing green waters; the solitary island with its pines; Sil-verhorn and Helmcrag; the ridge of Loughrigg, where the poet loved to walk; and, on the left, Rydal Water set like a jewel among the hills.

Between December, 1799, and May, 1808, while the Wordsworths were living in Dove Cottage, the poet composed " Michael," " The Cuckoo," " The Wanderer," " The Leech-ga- therer," " The Butterfly "—which describes the orchard-garden—" The Daisy," " Alice Fell," " The Beggars," the " Ode to Duty," " The Waggoner," " The Character of the Happy Warrior," " The White Doe of Rylstone." Here the great Ode on Immortality was begun, and here " The Prelude " and " The Excur- sion " were largely written. In the seclusion of this tiny garden Wordsworth's poetic prime was reached, and here his genius touched its highest mark of expression.

In 1808 the cottage became too small for the growing family, and the Wordsworths removed to Allan Bank, a larger house at the north end of Grasmere. From thence, in 1811, another move was made to the Rectory, a very charm- ing place opposite the church and within sound of the swiftly running Rotha. Here sorrow lived with the Wordsworths and became their familiar companion. Of their five children two died under this roof: Catherine, whom De Quincey loved with such intensity of ardor that he was terribly shaken by her sudden death— " never, from the foundation of these mighty hills," he wrote, " was there so fierce a convulsion of grief as mastered my faculties on receiving that heart-shattering news"; and Thomas, who followed his sister after a brief interval. Wordsworth's grief was, after the manner of the man, deep and passionate; forty years later he could not speak of these sorrows of his early life without agitation and suffering. The children sleep in the churchyard across the narrow road from the Rectory, and the associations of the place so weighed upon the poet's spirit that another and final removal was made in the spring of 1813 to Rydal Mount.

Few houses have been described so often, and none more perfectly matches the picture of a poet's home as the imagination instinctively conceives it. Standing on the rocky side of Nab Scar, above Rydal Lake, almost concealed by the vines which have grown apparently into its very structure, its terraces rich in hedges and foliage, Rydal Mount is a type of English repose, maturity, and natural loveliness. As one walks up the quiet road past the little church, the stir and turmoil of life are so distant and alien that one wonders if they be not the dreams of a disordered mind. Here are silence, seclusion, fathomless depths of greenness, enchanting beauty of glancing water and wandering mountain line.

At Rydal Mount " The Excursion " was finished, and " Laodamia," the " Evening Ode," " Yarrow Revisited," and the series of Ecclesiastical Sonnets written. The magical quality, the inimitable charm, of the " Daffodils," the " Solitary Reaper," the " Cuckoo," had vanished, the didactic note had become more distinct; but in his happiest hours the poet still had command of a noble style. Mr. Myers has noted the striking and beautiful close of Wordsworth's poetic life. It was in 1818 when Nature seemed to take solemn farewell of the genius which she had inspired, and which had, in turn, been her interpreter. There came one of those sunsets sometimes seen among the Cambrian hills, the splendors of which not only

Derwentwater

pass quite beyond speech, but impress even the unimaginative as almost apart from the ordinary processes of Nature. The earth and the sky, in the radiance of shifting cloud and folding mist, seem to blend together into a new and unspeakably wonderful world of light and color and spiritual splendor. Under the spell of that vision the poet's imagination rose once more to its earlier level in the " Evening Ode, composed on an evening of extraordinary splendor and beauty":

> No sound is uttered, but a deep
>   And solemn harmony pervades
> The hollow vale from steep to steep,
>   And penetrates the glades.
> Far distant images draw nigh,
>   Called forth by wondrous potency
> Of beamy radiance, that imbues
> Whate'er it strikes with gem-like hues!
>   In vision exquisitely clear
> Herds range along the mountain side;
> And glistening antlers are descried,
>   And gilded flocks appear.

The poet seemed to recognize the decline of his poetic power, the hardening of his faculties; for he adds, with pathetic clearness of insight:

THE LAKE COUNTRY

Full early lost, and fruitlessly deplored;
　Which at this moment, on my waking sight,
Appears to shine, by miracle restored!
　My soul, though yet confined to earth,
　Rejoices in a second birth;
—'T is past, the visionary splendor fades;
And night approaches with her shades.

In 1843, on the death of Southey, Wordsworth was persuaded to accept the position of Poet Laureate, and nobly wore the honor through seven years of unbroken silence. And in this vine-embosomed house, in April, 1850, the end came. As he had lived, so he died, in simple but sublime repose. The stream of visitors who pour through the Grasmere churchyard cannot destroy the spell of solemn silence which enfolds the poets' corner in that beautiful place of death and life. The old church, the steep hill, the shining thread of waterfall, the silent curve and sweep of the Rotha, the tombs of the poets—for William, his wife, Dorothy, and Hartley Coleridge lie together in that sacred place—who is not the better for the sight and the memory of them!

The Lake Country is not only the natural

but the spiritual background of Wordsworth's poetry. That poetry was, with few important exceptions, written there; in very many instances it grew out of localities which have been accurately determined, or was suggested by incidents which are still remembered; so intimate, indeed, is the connection between the great mass of the shorter poems and the landscape and life of the region that the verse seems but the description and interpretation of landscape and life. In the longer poems passage after passage can be assigned to definite places or connected with persons and incidents. But in a still deeper and more spiritual sense was Wordsworth's imagination affected by the little world of mountain, lake, and cloud in which he lived. That country suggests and illustrates, in a marvelous way, the two distinctive characteristics of Wordsworth's poetry: clear, accurate sight of the fact, and the sudden expansion of the vision to take in its largest relations and its most far-reaching spiritual symbolism. Wordsworth's genius was notable for its twofold recognition of the familiar and the sublime in Nature, its closeness of observation and its clearness of imaginative insight, its scientific exactness and its poetic vision; if the phrase may be permitted, Wordsworth habitually saw both the human and the divine sides of Nature—the fragrant orchard at his door, and the last sublime reach of mountain as it fades into sky.

The Lake Country presents both these aspects of Nature. The mountains are not high, and yet they are touched with sublimity; the cattle browse on their grassy slopes, and yet infinity and eternity seem somehow embodied in them. They are both familiar and mysterious. More than this, they suggest in the most subtle way the play of the imagination. Through the upper Vales the mists continually roll in from the sea, and the whole country is enfolded in an atmosphere which brings with it all the magic of light and shade, all the mystery of shadow and distance and the commingling of sky and earth. Miracles of light and color are daily wrought among those hills; enchantments and spells are woven there which the imagination cannot escape. The real and the visionary continually intermingle. The atmosphere works such marvels that it becomes a visible type of the play and processes of the imagination. In that country, as in the poetry of its interpreter, there are always the solid mass, the definite outline, the substantial form; and there is also the finer and visionary world into which the real world seems to rise, and with which it seems to blend in a whole which is both perishable and imperishable, both material and spiritual: the unity of the seen and the unseen. No one understood this subtle quality of the Lake Country landscape better than Wordsworth, and no one has so clearly defined and described it as he in the following passage:

The rain here comes down heartily, and is frequently succeeded by clear, bright weather, when every brook is vocal and every torrent sonorous; brooks and torrents which are never muddy even in the heaviest floods. Days of unsettled weather, with partial showers, are very frequent; but the showers darkening or brightening as they fly from hill to hill are not less grateful to the eye than finely interwoven passages of gay and sad music are touching to the ear. Vapors exhaling from the lakes and meadows after sunrise in a hot season, or in moist weather brooding upon the heights, or descending towards the valleys with inaudible motion, give a visionary character to everything around them;

and are in themselves so beautiful as to dispose us to enter into the feelings of those simple nations (such as the Laplanders of this day) by whom they are taken for guardian deities of the mountains; or to sympathize with others who have fancied these delicate apparitions to be the spirits of their departed ancestors. Akin to these are fleecy clouds resting upon the hill-tops; they are not easily managed in picture, with their accompaniments of blue sky, but how glorious are they in nature! how pregnant with imagination for the poet!

Emerson's Home from the Orchard

EMERSON AND CONCORD

EMERSON AND CONCORD

MERSON was born in what has become one of the busiest sections of Boston; but when the future poet and thinker opened his eyes in this world, on the 25th day of May, 1803, it was in a Congregational parsonage " in the silence of retirement, yet in the center of the territory of the metropolis," where, to continue the words of his father, " we may worship the Lord our God." That was the lifelong occupation of Ralph Waldo Emerson, and it is interesting to note that from the beginning it was singularly free from conventions and forms of every kind. Nature is, to most men, a middle term between

God and man; to Emerson it was a common ground over which the Universal Spirit always brooded, and where the open-hearted might happen upon inspiring hours. He felt the sublimity of the Psalms of David, and the noble swell of the Te Deum, the ancient hymn which the centuries have sung, never left him cold; but his highest thoughts came to him in the broad silence of summer afternoons in the fields, or when the stars kept up the ancient splendor of the wintry heavens. "Boys," Dr. Holmes reports him as saying to two youths who were walking with him as they entered the wood, "here we recognize the presence of the Universal Spirit. The breeze says to us in its own language, How d'ye do? How d'ye do? and we have already taken our hats off and are answering it with our own How d'ye do? How d'ye do? And all the waving branches of the trees, and all the flowers, and the field of corn yonder, and the singing brook, and the insect, and the bird—every living thing and things we call inanimate feel the same divine universal impulse while they join with us, and we with them, in the greeting which is the salutation of the Universal Spirit." In the life of the author of "Wood-notes," as in that of the author of the great ode on "Intimations of Immortality," Nature was a background so intimately and reverently lived with that the work of both poets was not only colored but penetrated by it.

Favorable conditions conspired in Emerson's ancestry, birth, and childhood to make him peculiarly sensitive to the influence of star and field and wood, by familiarizing him with the simplest habits of life and centering his interest in the things of the mind. He was the child of a long line of highly educated and poorly paid ministers; men who had the tastes and resources of scholars, but whose ways of living were as frugal as the ways of the poorest farmers to whom they preached. "We are poor and cold, and have little meal, and little wood, and little meat," wrote his father at the close of his Harvard pastorate and on the eve of the removal to Boston, "but, thank God, courage enough."

The moral fiber of the stock was as vigorous as its life had been self-denying and abstemious; but it must not be imagined that the long line of ministers behind Emerson were pallid ascetics. When his father was on the verge of death, he wrote to a relative: " You will think me better, because of the levity with which this page is blurred. Threads of this levity have been interwoven with the entire web of my life." This touch of gayety could hardly be called levity; it was, rather, the overflow of a very deep spring in the hearts of a race of men and women who kept their indebtedness to external conditions at the lowest in order that they might possess and use freely the amplest intellectual and spiritual means. Again and again, in the simple but noble annals of this family, whose name was on the college roll in every generation, one comes upon the fruit of this kind of frugality of appetite in the fine use of common things, and, above all, in an intimate sense of access to Nature and the right to draw freely on her resources of beauty and power.

This ancestral heritage of simple fare and good books first comes to light in the little community with which the greatest of the long line

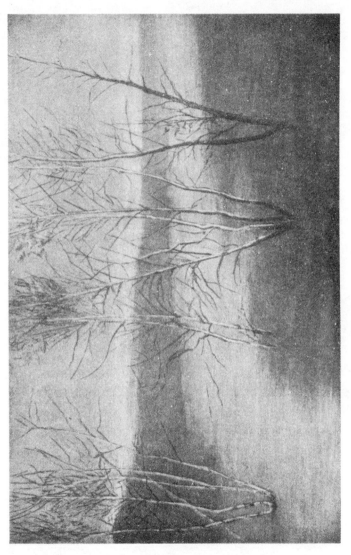

The Great Meadows

of scholars and teachers is so intimately associated that to think of "Nature" and "Wood-
notes " is to see Concord lying in quiet beauty
in a tranquil New England landscape. There
were Emersons in the pulpit in Ipswich and
Mendon, but it is upon Peter Bulkeley, grandfather at the seventh remove of Ralph Waldo,
that attention rests as typical ancestor. He
was descended, one of the oldest of the colonial
chronicles tells us, from an honorable family of
Bedfordshire; educated at St. John's College,
Cambridge, of the rich tone of whose second
quadrangle Ruskin spoke with enthusiasm; was
given a goodly benefice, but found himself later
unable to conform to the services of the English
Church; came to New England in 1635, and
after a brief stay in Cambridge " carried a good
Number of Planters with him, up further into
the *Woods,* where they gathered the *Twelfth
Church,* then formed in the Colony, and call'd
the Town by the name of Concord."

This pioneer scholar is described as a well-
read person, an exalted Christian, who had the
reverence not only of his own people but of all
sorts of people throughout the land, and espe-

cially of his fellow-ministers, who would still address him as a " Father, a Prophet, a Counsellor on all occasions." He had, we are told, " a competently good stroke at Latin Poetry," and he gave no small part of his library to Harvard College. William Emerson, who came five generations later, was as notable a leader in Concord as his great-great-grandfather had been. He preached the gospel of resistance to tyrants and practiced it as well; for he left the pulpit in Concord to join the army at Ticonderoga. When the miniature but immensely significant fight in which

> . . . the embattled farmers stood,
> And fired the shot heard round the world,

took place at the bridge, he stood on the steps of the Old Manse, which he had built ten years before, and was kept out of the fray only by the vigorous intervention of his friends.

In 1834, when Ralph Waldo Emerson was at the end of his period of apprenticeship, had withdrawn from the pulpit and made his first memorable trip to Europe, he went back to the Old Manse in Concord as to his ancestral home;

henceforth he was to know no other. His
grandfather, Dr. Ripley, sustained in the famous old house the best traditions of his race;
" he was a natural gentleman," wrote Emerson
in a charming character study; " no dandy, but
courtly, hospitable, manly, and public-spirited;
his nature social, his house open to all men.
His brow was serene and open to his visitor,
for he loved men, and he had no studies,
no occupations, which company could interrupt."

In September of the following year Emerson took his young wife to live in the house
which was to be his home to the end, and which
has become, by reason of its association with
him and his friends, one of the places which
both illustrate and interpret American life at
its best. The village of Concord was then the
quietest of rural communities; no trains connected it with Boston; no literary pilgrims visited it; no city folk had discovered it. It was
rich in historical associations; it had long been
the home of a small group of families of social
and intellectual distinction; the memories of its
heroic age were still fresh in the minds and

hearts of elderly people; but it did not stand out as yet on the map of the modern world. It was what Dr. Holmes would have called a Brahman town; in quality and dignity of character and habit it held a place by itself; and when, later, three or four men of genius made it famous, it seemed as if they had revealed Concord to the world rather than imparted to it a sudden prestige by reason of their residence there.

The country which was to be the background of Emerson's life and work was in such consonance with his temper and habits that, as in the case of Wordsworth and the English lake country, it is not fanciful to trace a real rather than an accidental relation and resemblance between the men and the landscapes they loved. In a very true sense, all history and all countries were behind Emerson's thought and work; he seemed to have the two hemispheres in his brain, one lobe being Oriental and the other Occidental. In certain moods he was of the East as distinctly as in the applications and urgency of his thought he was of the West. He was akin with Saadi in the breadth of his view and

The Pines of Walden

the catholicity of his experience; and he was
brother to Hafiz, not in physical delight in fragrance and melody, but in instinctive ease in
softening the hard line of the fact by evoking
its mystical significance. He was enamored of
Plato, and spoke of him with more warmth of
advocacy than was in his tones in urging the
claims of any other man of representative
genius. He valued the Roman power of or-
ganization; he felt the immense sense of reality
in Dante's symbolism of the experience of the
soul in the three worlds; he had read nearly all
the fifty-five volumes of Goethe that he owned
in the German, although he was never a
methodical reader, and he was in deep sympathy with Goethe's great contemporaries; and
he was at home in the wide range of English literature. He moved lightly through the store-
house of the past, with sound knowledge of
what it contained and with a sure instinct of
finding what was of value to him. He bor-
rowed generously, as he had a right, from the
capital of the race, and in every case he repaid
the loan at a high rate of interest.

Cosmopolitan as Emerson was in his interests, his surroundings, his tastes, he was nevertheless a true New Englander of the Concord quality. No one roamed further, but no one was a more devout home-keeper. He was eager to get the spiritual product, the deposit in the spirit, of the strain and storm of life; but he hugged his own hearth and was content to hear faint echoes of the tumult of life in the distance. A cosmopolitan in the range of his intelligence, he was a provincial in his habits and personal associations; and this was the prime characteristic of Concord. To a European it must have been a place of extraordinary contrasts; it was the home of the loftiest idealism and of the simplest manner of life. The little group of men and women of culture, among whom Emerson took his place by personal and hereditary right, shared this habit of 'rural or rustic simplicity with the farmer folk who surrounded them. In the old-fashioned farmhouses, which stood and still stand along the roads or hidden among trees in sheltered nooks, there was a mingled air of thrift and generosity. They were built on ample lines, and their frugality was tempered by hospitality.

The living was of the plainest; the mug of hard cider and the pot of beans were in every house; but there were also reverence, sobriety, respect for learning, the peace of God, and a love of liberty that had elements of passion in it.

"These poor farmers, who came up that day to defend their native soil," said Emerson in a memorable historical address, " acted from the simplest instincts; they did not know it was a deed of fame they were doing. These men did not babble of glory; they never dreamed their children would contend which had done the most. They supposed they had a right to their corn and their cattle—without paying tribute to any but their own Governors. And as they had no fear of man, they yet did have a fear of God." And he recalls the simple statement of one of these " embattled farmers " " that he went to the services of the day with the same seriousness and acknowledgment of God which he carried to the church." The spirit of the best in New England is revealed in these few words. They feared God, but they feared nothing else; they held to the highest truths in the simplest speech; and the best of them carried the world in their minds and stayed quietly at home. They had penetrated to the foundations; and although there was in Concord, as elsewhere in New England, an aristocracy of birth and intellect, men and women were honored on a basis of character.

This independence went so far that it sometimes became whimsical, as in Thoreau, and sometimes issued in such an excess of nonconformity that a man found it impossible to get on with his neighbors, and took refuge in isolation. The peculiarity of the New England hermit has not been his desire to get near to God, but his anxiety to get away from man. In later years, when Concord had become a Mecca, a whimsical self-consciousness was sometimes evident in the more individualistic members of the community. Alcott said that Thoreau thought he lived in the center of the universe and would annex the rest of the planet to Concord; while Thoreau's view of his own relation to the place is reflected in his confession: "Almost I believe the Concord would not rise and overflow its banks again were I not here." This note of superiority did not es-

The Elms of the Concord River

cape the keen-witted neighbors of Thoreau.
" Henry talks about Nature," said Madam
Hoar, " just as if she 'd been born and brought
up in Concord."

Emerson was the highest type of this mingled frugality of the life of the body and
generosity of the life of the mind; of this har-
monization of the highest and broadest interests
with the simplest domesticity. He took pleasure in dissociating the resources and distinction of the intellectual life from the conventions
and forms of an elaborate social life; and he
seemed to affect in dress and manner a slight
rusticity as heightening the effect of his
thought, as the slight hesitation in his speech
in public address brought out the marvelous felicity of his diction. He would not have disclaimed the compliment of being called the
" Yankee Plato " ; so entirely content was he to
be a resident of Concord as well as a citizen of
the world. In nothing was his soundness of
nature, his health of mind, more evident than
in the delicacy with which he protected himself
from the intimacy of some who were eager to
gain some personal possession of his thought,

and the gentle persistency with which he held unbalanced people at a distance and kept himself clear of all rash attempts to bring in the millennium prematurely.

Hawthorne has given us a characteristic report of the strange folk to be met in Concord in the days of the " newness " : " It was necessary to go but a little way beyond my threshold before meeting with stranger moral shapes of men than might have been encountered elsewhere in a circuit of a thousand miles. These hobgoblins of flesh and blood were attracted thither by the wide-spreading influence of a great original thinker, who had his earthly abode at the opposite extremity of our village. His mind acted upon other minds of a certain constitution with wonderful magnetism, and drew many men upon long pilgrimages to speak with him face to face. Young visionaries, to whom just so much insight had been imparted as to make life all a labyrinth around them, came to seek the clue that should guide them out of their self-involved bewilderment. Gray-headed theorists whose systems, at first air, had finally imprisoned them in an iron framework, traveled painfully to his door, not to ask deliverance, but to invite the free spirit into their own thralldom."

No one will ever know the annoyances, perplexities, and dangers of Emerson's position; what every one does know is that he never fell a victim to the countless illusions, delusions, and unbalanced dreams in which reproachful and perhaps impertinent followers, who misread his leading, endeavored to involve him. The foremost idealist of the New World, he rendered incalculable service to the cause he had at heart by holding it clean and clear above the touch of fanaticism, impracticable experiment, and the bitterness of the egoistical reformer. If he had committed the fortunes of Idealism to a disastrous venture, the loss to the youth of America would have been irreparable.

In April, 1824, two years before he took refuge in Concord, "stretched beneath the pines," Emerson wrote the poem which expresses the deepest instinct of his nature and the tranquillity and detachment he was to find in the quiet village:

79

EMERSON AND CONCORD

Good-bye, proud world! I 'm going home:
. . . .
I am going to my own hearthstone,
Bosomed in yon green hills alone,—
A secret nook in a pleasant land,
Whose groves the frolic fairies planned;
Where arches green, the livelong day,
Echo the blackbird's roundelay,
And vulgar feet have never trod
A spot that is sacred to thought and God.

O, when I am safe in my sylvan home,
I tread on the pride of Greece and Rome;
And when I am stretched beneath the pines,
Where the evening star so holy shines,
I laugh at the lore and the pride of man,
At the sophist schools and the learned clan;
For what are they all, in their high conceit,
When man in the bush with God may meet?

Emerson was in no sense a hermit; an invet-
erate traveler of the mind, he was, for his time,
an experienced traveler among his kind. His
trips to Europe were memorable by reason of
his quick and decisive insight, of which the
"English Traits" is a permanent record; and
by reason of what he brought back in broader
sympathies and clearer discernment of the
great race qualities. He was for many years

A Corner of the Study

a familiar and honored figure on the lyceum
platform in distant sections of the country, and
he came to have a wide knowledge of the
United States of the middle decades of the
nineteenth century. He had a keen appetite
for good talk, and he was often seen in Cambridge and Boston in social gatherings great
and small. But his genius was essentially
meditative; he brooded over his subjects until
they cleared themselves in his mind; he kept
himself in an attitude of invitation, and his
thoughts came to him; above all, his work was
the fruit of the ripening of his own nature, and
he needed alike the quiet of the fallow and of
the growing field. The solitude in which a man
finds himself and the silence in which his
thoughts come to him he found in Concord.

Tranquillity and peace were its possessions
by reason of its isolation and of the conformation of its landscape. Monadnock and Wachu-
sett stood on the horizon for those who went to
look at them; but Concord lay content along a
river of slumberous mood, with a group of pel-
lucid lakes or ponds within easy reach, with
broad meadows and low hills and stretches of

whispering pines at hand. It was a shire-town, and it had business relations with lumbermen and farmers who came to it for supplies. It was on the route of four stage lines, and under the roofs of as many taverns old-fashioned toddy was mixed for home consumption and as an expression of hospitality to guests and travelers. Thoreau noted in the quiet village all the signs of the ordinary uses and habits of men: " I observed that the vitals of the village were the grocery, the bar-room, the post-office, and the bank; and, as a necessary part of the machinery, they kept a bell, a big gun, and a fire-engine at convenient places, and the houses were so arranged as to make the most of mankind, in lanes and fronting one another, so that every traveler had to run the gauntlet, and every man, woman, and child might get a lick at him."

It must be remembered, however, that two houses within call made a crowded community for Thoreau, and that the appearance of a strange or inquisitive person on the highway sent him incontinently into the woods. Concord, in the thirties and forties, was an entirely normal village, with the usual conveniences for conducting life; but the life of the time was exceedingly deliberate in movement, and the passage of several stages a day did not make a fever in the blood of the villagers. Emerson found there seclusion without isolation, and solitude and silence tempered with the most congenial companionship.

The Old Manse, in which he lived for the first year, is a dignified old house, in a locality of heroic tradition, in a place of singularly reposeful beauty, in so quiet an air that one can easily overhear the whisperings of the pines. Under its roof generations of gentlefolk have lived frugally and in loyal devotion to the highest interests of the spirit; from colonial days books of classic quality have been within reach in the halls and rooms; in a small room on the second floor at the back of the house Hawthorne wrote a part of the " Mosses from an Old Manse " and Emerson wrote " Nature." When the latter appeared anonymously, the question, "Who is the author of ' Nature ' ? " brought out the reply, " God and Ralph Waldo Emerson."

If tranquillity is the distinctive note of Concord, a tinge of something dim and shadowy seems to touch the Old Manse and impart to it, not gloom nor sadness, but something of the twilight effect of the pine groves. When one recalls its traditions of plain living and high thinking, one is reminded of Dove Cottage; but the little stone cottage embosomed in foliage where Wordsworth spent the most productive decade of his life is now a shrine set apart to memory, while the Old Manse is still a home from which in these later years has come pictorial genius of a high order; and the impulses which have made Concord a place apart have not spent their force.

In this rural community, snugly at home in a landscape full of repose, Emerson found the best conditions for his growth and work, and through his long life lived on most intimate terms with his nearest and most companionable neighbor, Nature. " Hail to the quiet fields of my fathers," he wrote when he had settled himself in the Old Manse. " Not wholly unattended by supernatural friendship and favor let me come hither. Bless my purposes as they are simple and virtuous. . . . Henceforth I

Early Morning at the Old Manse

design not to utter any speech, poem, or book
that is not entirely and peculiarly my work. I
will say, at public lectures and the like, those
things which I have meditated for their own
sake and not for the first time with a view to
that occasion." In these words is to be found
the secret of his relation to Concord and of his
beautiful and fruitful life; he came to Nature
as to the word of God, and he gave the world
only the ripe fruit of his quiet, meditative, con-
secrated life. The twin activities of his spirit
found their field and their inspiration under the
open sky. He played with Nature and she
worked with him. With him, as with Wordsworth, his working-room was out-doors; his
writing-room was the place where he made a
record of his hours and studies under the open
sky. No season barred the woods to his eager
feet; he was abroad in winter as in summer, and
he loved lonely walks at night, finding companionship with the stars full of inspiration.

The pine woods brought him some of his happiest moods and many of his most felicitous
thoughts and phrases. In all weathers he went
abroad alert and expectant, waiting serenely

and confidently on the ancient oracles; and, holding himself in this trustful, receptive attitude, the pines became for him

Pipes through which the breath of God doth blow
A momentary music.

Thoreau, keen observer though he was, took into the woods a personality which affected his vision and made him the most conspicuous object in the landscape; Emerson left himself at home and brought to Nature the most receptive and impersonal of moods. He saw fewer things than Thoreau, but he saw more deeply. " But if I go into the forest," he wrote, " I find all new and undescribed; nothing has been told me. The screaming of wild geese was never heard; the thin note of the titmouse and his bold ignoring of the bystander; the fall of the flies that patter on the leaves like rain; the angry hiss of some bird that crepitated at me yesterday; the formation of turpentine, and, indeed, every vegetation and animation, any and all, are alike undescribed. Every man that goes into the woods seems to be the first man that ever went into a wood. His sensations and his world are new. You really think that nothing can be said about morning and evening, and the fact is, morning and evening have not yet begun to be described. When I see them I am not reminded of these Homeric or Miltonic or Shakespearian or Chaucerian pictures, but I feel a pain of an alien world, or I am cheered with the moist, warm, glittering, budding, and melodious hour that takes down the narrow walls of my soul and extends its pulsation and life to the very horizon. That is Morning; to cease for a bright hour to be the prisoner of this sickly body and to become as large as the World."

Compare this account of the attitude which Emerson took toward Nature with the fragrant, dewy, glowing account of a day under the pure sky which Corot left among his records, and the secret of spiritual and artistic vitality and freshness is plain. The men of genius, who recreate life in art to assuage the thirst and renew the heart of the world, are immortal not only in their works but in themselves; for they are the children of God, playing in a world in which their fellows toil. It is their happy lot to see all things afresh and keep the world young.

There was a garden on the south side of the Emerson house, and apple-trees brought the most ancient fragrance and domestic associations to the place; but Emerson was more at home in the broad landscape which inclosed his own acres. What the old road over the hill to Grasmere and Loughrigg Terrace were to Wordsworth in the long years at Rydal Mount, the Great Fields and Meadows, the shores and groves of white pine about Walden Pond, Peters Field, and the level stretches through which the Musketaquid, most quiet of rivers, flows, were to Emerson during the most fruitful period of his life. He found endless delight in the ownership of a tract of land from which he could look down on Walden Pond and away to the farther hills:

> My garden is a forest ledge
>   Which older forests bound;
> The banks slope down to the blue lake-edge,
>   Then plunge to depths profound.

Walden Ledge by Moonlight

EMERSON AND CONCORD

Self-sown my stately garden grows;
  The wind, and wind-blown seed,
Cold April rain and colder snows,
  My hedges plant and feed.

Emerson was not a successful farmer,
though he had the respect of the practical
farmers about him, and was known as " a first-
rate neighbor and one who always kept his
fences up " ; his business was not with the acres,
but with the landscape. No one ever took ampler or nobler harvests of the spirit off the land
than Emerson. He had a keen eye for the
small facts of natural life, but he cared
chiefly for the vital processes, the flooding life,
the revelation of truth, the correspondence of
soul between man and Nature; he was, in a
word, the poet in the woods and fields. With
serene faith and loyal fellowship he kept
friends with Nature from youth to age, and the
joy of his intimacy suffered no shadow of es-
trangement as the years went by. A walk in
the woods, he declared, was " one of the secrets
for dodging old age " ; and in an address " To
the Woods " he wrote: " Whoso goeth in your
paths readeth the same cheerful lesson, whether

he be a young child or a hundred years old. . . .
Give me a tune like your winds or brooks or
birds, for the songs of men grow old, when they
are uprooted; but yours, though a man have
heard them for seventy years, are never the
same, but always new, like Time itself, or like
love."

To the very end this devout lover of Nature
lived in daily intercourse with her, and it was
during a walk in a cold April rain that he con-
tracted the illness which proved fatal after a
few days of sitting in his chair by the fire calmly
waiting for death. In the quiet place where he
lies, near Hawthorne and Thoreau, the pines
seem to be always whispering among themselves; but, alas! there is no longer one who understands them.

Sunnyside

THE WASHINGTON IRVING
COUNTRY

THE WASHINGTON IRVING COUNTRY

RVING and Longfellow were primarily translators and interpreters of the Old World to the New; to them was due in large measure the liberation of the young nation from provincialism, not by the use of fresh motives or of novel literary forms, but by bringing the American imagination in touch with the imagination of Europe, and reknitting the deeper ties which had been, in a way, severed by forcible separation from Old World rule. There was, in the first three decades of the nineteenth century, general dependence on European literature and general defer-

ence to European taste; a dependence from
which Emerson and Poe, by definite and urgent
teaching as well as by practice of art with that
freshness and force which always form another
beginning, finally effected our liberation.

This deferential attitude, this imitative spirit,
had nothing in common with that assimilation
of the experience, sentiment, poetic association,
and historic charm of the older civilization which
Irving and Longfellow effected. They assisted
in the emancipation from servile imitation by
greatly forwarding the equalization of the conditions of culture between the Old World and
the New, and by bringing the New into spiritual
sympathy with the Old. This work was different from that of Emerson and Poe, but Irving
and Longfellow share the distinction of breaking the formal while reuniting the vital ties, and
thus preparing the way for the free interchange
of influence on a basis of equality which to-day
constitutes the rich spiritual commerce between
the Old World and the New. To this great end
Cooper was also a strenuous and effective
worker; failing dismally when he tried the rôle
of interpreter in " Precaution," succeeding on

The Entrance to Sleepy Hollow

original lines when he portrayed the fresh experiences and characteristic types of the new society in " The Spy " and " The Leatherstocking Tales."

But while Irving and Longfellow were translators in a high sense and with fresh feeling of the Old World to the New, they were also original forces in the literature of the new country. Their urbanity, geniality, hospitality of mind, and sweetness of nature gave them rare sensitiveness of feeling for things old and ripe and beautiful and a winning quality of style; qualities which, among a people whose literature, during its first important period, was to carry suggestions of the pulpit with it, have tended somewhat to obscure their originality and significance. Longfellow was so gentle a preacher that, aside from a few poems so frankly didactic that we forgive their exhortations for the sake of the pure impulse they convey, the bands and gown are concealed under the singer's robes; while Irving's preaching was wholly the silent influence of one of the finest, kindliest, and truest of men. In the preponderance of ethical over artistic interests in this country Longfellow and Irving have carried less weight and made less impression than writers of more urgent ethical impulse but of far less poetic and literary power. When a great deal of current writing has been forgotten, and much that Irving and Longfellow wrote has passed into the same oblivion, it is safe to predict that " The Legend of Sleepy Hollow " and " Rip Van Winkle," and " Evangeline " and " Hiawatha," will hold their own because of their quality as literature and because they are part of the very limited legendary lore of America. Irving gave permanent form to the Knickerbocker tradition when he created Diedrich Knickerbocker and Rip Van Winkle; and in " The Legend of Sleepy Hollow " he was not only the forerunner of the American novelist but the first American mythmaker.

Like Longfellow and Cooper, he was often in Europe; and it may be suspected that when these writers were young, and for a long time after, the new country was a lonely place for men who craved richness and beauty of life, the charm of old association, the ripeness of a society which had gotten through with foundation-laying, had

106

built its roads, and had passed on to love things which are beautiful as well as to do things which are useful.

Born in 1783, in the cosmopolitan city of New York, where even at that early period eighteen or twenty languages were spoken, Irving went to Europe in search of health in his twenty-second year; saw something of France, Italy, Holland, and England; enjoying with the freshness of a young imagination nature, art, society, and life. " I am a young man and in Paris," he wrote to a friend at home. Returning to New York in 1806, he took his place at once in the little group of wits and men-about-town, in the good sense of the phrase, of which Paulding, Brevoort, Henry Ogden, and the Kembles were members—a spirited, vivacious company, with great capacity for enjoyment and with gifts of humor and satire which, under the influence of Goldsmith, Addison, and the eighteenth-century essayists, were soon at work in the little city " to instruct the young, inform the old, correct the town, and castigate the age," to quote from " Salmagundi," which ran its meteoric course in twenty numbers and then vanished in the mystery from which it had come. When "The History of New York by Diedrich Knickerbocker" appeared, it reminded Walter Scott of Dean Swift and of Sterne.

In 1815 Irving went to Europe for the second time, and seventeen years passed before he set foot in his native city again. During this period he wrote "The Sketch-Book," a collection of essays in his most characteristic vein, urbane, genial, full not only of Old World atmosphere, Old World grace, ease, mellowness of reflection, and sentiment, but full also of New World feeling. "Bracebridge Hall" brought the fragrance of old gardens and the dignity of old homes once more to the children of the men and women who had left them behind two centuries before; "The Tales of a Traveler," which appeared two years later and was read with eager interest, dealt with old things, but was full of novelty to the untraveled America of the third decade of the last century. "The Life of Columbus" was begun, and "The Tales of the Alhambra" and "The Conquest of Granada" were finished, during this long residence abroad; and when he returned, in 1832, Irving's most

On Sleepy Hollow Brook

characteristic work was done. He was still to write " The Life of Washington," " Mahomet and his Successors," the charming account of Goldsmith, and other books; but he struck no new notes and disclosed no new qualities as a writer.

At first glance it would seem as if Irving's work had been done against many backgrounds, English and Spanish as well as American, and as if his note had been cosmopolitan rather than American. The real Irving, however, was a true son of the country of which New York is the capital, and his characteristic and abiding work had behind it a city, a river, and a mountain range which were not simply the stage setting of his life, but which gave color, atmosphere, tone, to his writing. As a translator Irving rendered a great service to his country, and enriched its literature with the meditations on Westminster Abbey, the description of Stratford-on-Avon, and the group of studies of English life and landscape in " Bracebridge Hall "; but the Irving who will be known to the future will be the Geoffrey Crayon of the Knickerbocker city, and the books which will

111

live longest, because they are in material and manner most completely his own, will be the legends of the Hudson.

His kindly and pervasive humor had as little in common with the keen, pungent New England humor as his genial and urbane spirit had with the strenuous, ethical temper of New England. The rigidity of the Puritan, the concentration of the reformer, were entirely alien to his tolerant nature. The intense feeling for the locality, the emphasis on the section, characteristic of the South from a very early period, were equally alien to him. He was a true child of the metropolis; tolerant in temper because he was on easy terms with many different races, urbane and gracious because he had found virtue in many kinds of men, charm in many kinds of women, and sincerity in many kinds of religion; with a vein of deep and tender feeling running through his nature and his work, but always relieving the strain of emotion with that touch of humor which makes men kin. The qualities of the cosmopolitan city were all his: urbanity of manner, breadth of view, tolerance of temper, and a kindly, easy, genial attitude towards life.

WASHINGTON IRVING COUNTRY

The atmosphere of the New York of the first quarter of the nineteenth century penetrates Irving's work as thoroughly as the air of Ayrshire breathes through the songs of Burns, as the lonely loveliness and the wild ruggedness of Trossachs and lakes appear and vanish and reappear in picture and vision in Scott's prose and verse, and the multitudinous murmur of waters of Cumberlandshire is heard in the poems of Wordsworth.

There was no strain of didacticism in Irving, but there was an attitude towards life which gave his work a beautiful quality of sympathy. " If, however, I can by a lucky chance, in these days of evil, rub out one wrinkle from the brow of care, or beguile the heavy heart of one moment of sadness; if I can, now and then, penetrate the gathering film of misanthropy, prompt a benevolent view of human nature, and make my reader more in good humor with his fellow-beings and himself, surely, surely I shall not then have written in vain."

This is the temper of the true citizen of a metropolis—a place where races meet and mingle on easy terms; slowly and often blindly, but

none the less surely, through mutual comprehension and the tolerance that comes from it,
defining in terms of experience the unity of the
race and realizing the brotherhood of man. And
it was still in the cosmopolitan temper that Irving wrote to a friend: "I have preferred ad-
dressing myself to the feelings and fancy of the
reader more than to his judgment. My writings
may appear, therefore, light and trifling in our
country of philosophers and politicians. But
if they possess merit in the class of literature
to which they belong, it is all to which I aspire
in the work."

There was something of this breadth of humor, this love of literature for itself and not
as a tool for the preacher and the reformer, this
old-fashioned, kindly, easy-going metropolitan
temper, in the aspect and bearing of the man.
"Forty years ago," writes Mr. Curtis, "upon
a pleasant afternoon, you might have seen trip-
ping with an elastic step along Broadway, in
New York, a figure which even then would have
been called quaint. It was a man of about sixty-
six or sixty-seven years old, of a rather solid
frame, wearing a Talma, as a short coat of the

Old Willows near Tarrytown

time was called, that hung from the shoulders, and low shoes, neatly tied, which were observable at a time when boots were generally worn. The head was slightly inclined to one side, the face was smoothly shaven, and the eyes twinkled with kindly humor and shrewdness. There was a chirping, cheery, old-school air in the whole appearance, an undeniable Dutch aspect, which, in the streets of New Amsterdam, irresistibly recalled Diedrich Knickerbocker. . . . This modest and kindly man was the creator of Diedrich Knickerbocker and Rip Van Winkle. He was the father of our literature and at that time its patriarch."

New York was a little city of about twenty-five thousand inhabitants, living well below the site of the present City Hall, when Irving was born in a house on William Street, between Fulton and John, and christened in St. George's Chapel in Beekman Street. He went to school in Ann and Fulton streets, but he was given more to wandering about the pier-heads and watching incoming and outgoing ships in fair weather than to orderly study. He came to know the little city intimately in its most characteristic aspects and localities; for the loitering of an imaginative boy is a golden opportunity of getting at the heart of things. In this same blissful mood, while the mind was still much more concerned with the face of the world than with its own thoughts, he explored the secluded and solitary recesses of Sleepy Hollow and felt the quieting beauty of Tappan Zee on summer afternoons. A little later he made his first voyage up the Hudson on a sloop—a voyage which was then more unusual and exciting than a voyage across the Atlantic is to-day, and quite as long:

visit

" Of all the scenery of the Hudson," he wrote years afterwards, " the Kaatskill Mountains had the most witching effect on my boyish imagination. Never shall I forget the effect on me of my first view of them predominating over a wide extent of country, part wild, woody, and rugged; part softened away into all the graces of cultivation. As we slowly floated along, I lay on the deck and watched them through a long summer's day, undergoing a thousand mutations under the magical effects of atmosphere; sometimes seeming to approach, at other times to recede; now almost melting into hazy distance, now burnished by the setting sun, until in the evening they printed themselves against the glowing sky in the deep purple of an Italian land-

118

scape. . . . To me the Hudson is full of storied associations, connected as it is with some of the happiest portions of my life. Each striking feature brings to mind some early adventure or enjoyment; some favorite companion who shared it with me; some fair object, perchance, of youthful admiration, who, like a star, may have beamed her allotted time and passed away."

This first voyage up the river with which he will always be associated was as truly a voyage of discovery as was Hendrik Hudson's in 1609; and it was the river in its entirety, its large lines, its atmosphere, rather than its details of curving shore and climbing hill, the sweep of its powerful tide, that took possession of the boy's imagination, and became as much a part of his life of the mind and of his work as the mountains about Cadore were a part of the mind and work of Titian. It was not until April, 1835, that he purchased Sunnyside, that secluded and fragrant spot where he found such peace in his later years; and " Rip Van Winkle " had been published twelve years before its author set foot in the country which he had described more vitally than any other traveler has ever done.

From the early days of his dreaming boyhood

119

Irving knew the river in its large outlines, its noble molding of shore, its harmony of different types of landscape composed in one great picture, its atmosphere and its associations. " Rip Van Winkle " and " The Legend of Sleepy Hollow," the most original and characteristic of Irving's creations, were written in England during the period when he was transcribing with a sensitive and sympathetic hand the ripe loveliness of the English country and the rich associations of ancient structures and localities; but the Hudson valley, from the city at its conflux with the Bay to the fastnesses of the Catskills, was the background against which his imagination was working, because it was the background of his childhood.

It is now, perhaps, somewhat a matter of association, but there is a certain congruity between Irving's work and his country. In his attitude towards his fellows, his bearing in the world, Geoffrey Crayon bore the impress of the little metropolis which he has made for all time the city of the Knickerbockers; for, although Diedrich Knickerbocker has never been seen since he climbed into the Albany stage leaving

Along Sleepy Hollow Brook on the Old Philipse Manor

his bill at the tavern unpaid, he has left his name
and the tradition of his quaint personality to
the great metropolis to-day as its one touch of
mythology—a bit of fable symbolical of a past
which has been buried under crushing masses of
stone and iron. In the free play of Irving's imagination, in the geniality of his humor, in the
ease and leisureliness of his mood, the characteristics of the larger background of his life are
constantly suggested. If the Puritans had discovered the Hudson and turned its shores and
current to thrifty account, it might have suggested movement, energy, the stir of active
races; it suggests instead repose, quietness, long
summer days of a temperature which predis-
poses to acceptance of what fortune brings
rather than resolute grappling with adverse
conditions. Sunnyside wears its name, after all
these years and changes, with gracious assur-
ance. Approached by a long shaded lane and
embowered by trees, it still looks the summer in
the face in the broad expanse of Tappan Zee.

It was a happy stroke of felicitous description
which called the quiet little vale where the Po-
cantico takes its rise Sleepy Hollow; a place as

123

reposeful, after all these bustling and hurrying years, as it was in the days when Irving first described its pastoral somnambulance; a place not so much for meditation as for those reveries which come between sleep and awakening and add the charm of consciousness to the sensuous delight of sleep.

And although the Catskills have mass and nobility of line which produce an impression out of proportion to their actual magnitude, they have friendliness of aspect, an air of quiet hospitality, a something which eludes analysis, which imposes respect and yet invites familiarity. On summer afternoons they seem to sleep against the western sky; and a well-known artist, who has lived with them on terms of intimacy for many years, is in the habit of saying that they frame the most magnificent sunsets in the world. They stand revealed in their mystery of noble repose only in the hours when the shadows lengthen and the light loses its garishness; they are most expressive in the afternoon, when they seem sometimes to float in a mist of heat and to bound the horizon of the actual like noble visions of a world in which the light flows like molten gold. The White Mountains become bolder in the high light of morning, and invite strenuous approach and hint at great, positive rewards for the climber.

In October the Catskills hold the very genius of the season in their keeping; so deep is the quiet that enfolds them, so rich the atmosphere in which they lie, removed at times as in a radiant mirage and again distinct in softened line and golden distance.

Mr. Curtis has said, in pardonable poetic phrase, that the Rhine is lyrical and the Hudson epical. The Rhine is beautiful in localities, romantic, picturesque, entirely apart from their manifold associations. The Hudson is beautiful in its totality, its sustained interest, its singular harmony in diversity, its impressive continuity of changing landscapes blending into a nobly composed picture. The Rhine has a swift current and gives one a sense of movement and agitation; the Hudson flows so quietly that its very motion seems part of the stillness. On a summer day the voyage which Irving made as a boy with kindling imagination can be made between dawn and sunset, and takes one through

125

a valley in which it seems to be always afternoon. There is activity of many kinds on either bank and on the surface of the river, but in the spaciousness of stream and landscape the hum and stir are resolved into all-embracing silence, and the quietness of Sleepy Hollow broods over wooded shores, distant hills, and flowing water.

The acquaintance with the Hudson made when Irving was a boy was renewed and deepened when he finally returned from Europe in 1832, after an absence of seventeen years. New York had grown into what seemed to him a vast city; a few years later he described it in a letter to a friend as a "great crowded metropolis . . . full of life, bustle, noise, show, and splendor, . . . one of the most racketing cities in the world." One wonders what he would think of the roaring vortex of life which the slow little town of the forties, when this description was written, has become in these times of rebuilding on a scale which would have appalled the magicians of "The Arabian Nights."

Sunnyside was already old when he made it a retreat from the tumult of the city and began the process of enlargement which has adapted

The Old Dutch Church in Sleepy Hollow Cemetery

the ancient house to modern needs without sacri-
ficing its old-time charm. " My own place has
never been so beautiful as at present," he wrote
years later. " I have made more openings by
pruning and cutting down trees, so that from
the piazza I have several charming views of the
Tappan Zee and the hills beyond, all set, as it
were, in verdant frames; and I am never tired
of sitting there in my old Voltaire chair, of a
long summer morning, with a book in my hand,
sometimes reading, sometimes musing, and
sometimes dozing, and mixing up all in a pleasant dream." A beautiful picture, surely, of
the old age of a man of letters who continued
the tradition of the ripeness of spirit, the meditative temper, geniality, and humor, which has
never lapsed among the English-speaking
peoples.

In those years when the Albany stages were
making their last trips and the mild thunder of
the first railroad trains began to wake the echoes
of the Highlands and disturb the slumbers of
the Rip Van Winkles who have never been lacking in the old towns of Dutch origin, Irving was
enriching the Hudson with literary and personal

129

associations and making it a place of pilgrimage,
but his own associations with it lay far back in
his boyhood. In the later years it was the background of his personal life; in his early years it
was the background of his life of imagination
and sentiment, of his dawning consciousness of
his gifts and his vocation, of his gentle and re-
sponsive but essentially robust spirit. He lived
at Sunnyside, he worshiped at Christ Church in
the beautiful old village of Tarrytown, and he
lies at rest in Sleepy Hollow Cemetery: these
are the obvious associations of the man with the
country which will long bear his name. To find
his deeper and more vital connections with the
Hudson valley one must go back to his youth, to
his earlier books, to the heart of his work. Its
beauty, always reposeful and in summer touched
with elusive dreaminess, went home to his young
imagination and reappeared again and again in
charming description, in two legends which have
taken their places among our classics, not only
because of the charm of their form, but because
they are penetrated with the very spirit of the
region they portray, and in the quietness, the
sensitiveness to old associations, the charity for

that ease which the strenuous New England temper called by another name, the pervading humor which is never obtrusive or boisterous but is full of heart and fellowship, the happy blending of dignity and graciousness, and the modulated cadence of English speech in his work.

In the long future there may come a Hudson of new associations; a river freighted with the traffic of a valley which has become a continuous city from its mouth to the foothills of the Adirondacks. In that day some writer may appear whose work will echo the multitudinous voices of countless factories and the murmur of a vast population. But for many a year to come the Hudson which Hendrik explored as the herald of a host of sturdy Dutch settlers, the Hudson of long decades of slumberous plenty, of stately and humble homes—the Hudson of three centuries—will flow through Irving's country, and remain typical of his genius; the background of his art and life.

Goethe's House

WEIMAR AND GOETHE

WEIMAR AND GOETHE

HE one hundred and fifty-fourth anniversary of the birth of Goethe, which fell on the 28th day of last August, found Weimar not only eager to honor the memory of the great poet who was for fifty-six years its best-known resident, and is likely to remain to the end of time its most illustrious citizen, but essentially unchanged since his death in 1832. Even in a quiet German town, off the great highways of travel, changes must come in seventy-one years; and if Goethe were to step out of his old home to-day and walk to the grand-ducal palace, rebuilt in part under his own direction, he would doubtless

come upon unfamiliar sights. But Weimar remains in essentials a town of the old time: quaint, thoroughly German, and rich in association, not only with great men, but with some of the earliest statements of the modern conception of the relation of art to life.

The little town is preëminently fitted to be the custodian of literary traditions. It has an old-time dignity of bearing, as if it had always been the mother of great spirits. The quiet Ilm, flowing through its domain, is sacredly guarded along its entire course on both shores by a charming park; the homes of the poets are piously regarded; and there are worthy memorials of greatness in public places. The statue of Herder, one of the purest and most penetrating of modern minds, stands in front of the Stadt-Kirche, and bears his favorite and very characteristic motto, *Licht, Liebe, Leben;* in front of the theater Goethe and Schiller are commemorated in a noble group; the Grand Duke Augustus, in an equestrian statue, wears the laurel secured for him by the great spirits whom he had the sagacity to recognize and bring into his service; while Wieland is remembered in the fine salon which bears his name in the palace.

One may spend many hours with profit in Goethe's house, now restored as nearly as possible to the condition in which the poet left it: a fine house, notable chiefly for the range of interests expressed in the collections of several kinds which it contains, and for the evidence which it gives of the mingled dignity and simplicity of the poet's life—the first expressed in spacious rooms given over to pictures, busts, and memorials of great men, and the second disclosed by the extreme plainness of the working-room, and the tiny chamber opening from it in which Goethe died. It is profitable to walk through the palace and study the elegant salons in which Goethe and Schiller are commemorated by mural scenes from their works, and then go directly to the simple little rooms, not far distant, in which the two poets died; or to enter the grand-ducal vault in the new cemetery and note the presence of wreaths and flowers on the coffins, not of princely rulers, but of the two poets, whose beautiful friendship finds here its final expression.

WEIMAR AND GOETHE

Best of all, perhaps, is it to walk through the winding, shaded park, barely kept from wildness; to come in a secluded place upon the coiled serpent in bronze which symbolized for Goethe the *genius loci;* to make one's way slowly to the garden house which Goethe loved so well, and in which he so often sought solitude and silence for his work, and to sit in the places which were dear to him. Never, surely, did a meditative spirit find more congenial surroundings than Goethe found in these green and fragrant places of peace. It is a piece of special good fortune to fall in, along those walks, as did the writer, with an old-time resident of Weimar who has grown up in its traditions and loves it for its poets, and to hear his eager, affectionate narrative of events and story of localities; and then to go into some secluded spot and ask one's self what there was in Goethe's career and genius to justify the extraordinary interest which centers in him.

The minor conditions in Goethe's life were unusually fortunate, for the poet was well born in every sense; his childhood had surroundings picturesque to the eye and full of suggestion to

Goethe's Working-room

the imagination; he had exceptional educational opportunities, the best and most fruitful of them being his mother's genius for story-telling; he had perfect health and an impressive and winning personality; he never knew care in the ordinary sense of the word, for he was all his life shielded from material uncertainty and anxiety, with work enough of the methodical kind to give him occupation and position, but not enough to diminish the energy of his intelligence or to destroy the freshness of his spirit. He had rank, station, friends, fame, and long life—all great and helpful aids to the unfolding and maturing of a great nature and the free flow outward of a great inward force. These prosperous conditions were important, but they were, nevertheless, minor conditions; for they did not bear directly upon the impulse which a creative nature receives from rich material, from a stirring atmosphere, and from that searching appeal to the heart and the imagination made by a great people silent but full of spiritual eagerness and restless with unexpressed thought and emotion.

Homer spoke to a homogeneous race; Dante

to a divided country, but to an Italian nature, alert, energetic, and proudly conscious of the possession of great qualities; Shakespeare to an England turbulent, ill-conditioned, and untrained in the higher arts, but overflowing with unspent vitality, with a dawning national consciousness full of insolence, but full also of splendid possibilities of growth and achievement. In Goethe's youth there was not only no Germany, but there was, in the deepest sense of the phrase, no German people. There was a multitude of petty States, but there was no nation; there were Prussians, Hanoverians, Saxons, Bavarians, Swabians, but there was, for the purposes of art, no German race. There was a country held together by geographical conditions, but split into fragments by political boundary lines; there was a race of common origin, but broken asunder by differences of religion, of history, temperament, and ideal; there was a language common to a large community, but still to be enriched by the loving genius of great artists, who are constantly adding to the resources of speech no less than to those of thought. There had been true poets in Germany centuries before Goethe, and the literature was rich in legend and tradition, in epic and song, but it is nevertheless true that there had been no great German literature. Goethe was the contemporary in his old age of Scott and Carlyle, but there was no Chaucer, Shakespeare, Spenser, Milton, or Dryden behind him; there were in place of these the old Epic poets; there were Hans Sachs, Klopstock, and Wieland. The significance of this statement lies in the fact that, although the German language was as old as the English, it had no great poets. It is true that Homer and Dante had no great predecessors, but each stood at the beginning of the real history of his race; Goethe, on the other hand, appeared at a late hour in that history, and found the literature still to be created, and the language still to be modulated to the finer uses of expression. Youth was past, both for the race and the people, but the works of youth were still to be accomplished and the fruits of youth were still to be borne.

There were great figures in Germany while Goethe was a student at Leipsic and at Strassburg; but Lessing, Herder, and Winckelmann were thinkers and critics of the creative temper rather than writers of the creative order and quality. The names of Bodmer and Gottsched, those wooden gods of a Germany in artistic and intellectual tutelage to France, bring before the mind by concrete illustration the aridity of spirit, the shallowness of insight, and the deadness of thought which reigned in Germany in the early years of Goethe's life. Never has a poet of the first rank fallen upon times more uninspiring and come to maturity among a people more divided. Both race and language were old, but they lacked the trained intelligence, the solidarity of experience, the unity of emotion and ideal, which are the finest fruits of maturity.

From the very start Goethe was driven back upon himself and forced to undertake consciously and of set purpose the work which, under more inspiring conditions, would have been almost instinctive. For to speak simply and naturally, in good German speech out of a sound German heart, was, at the time " Götz " appeared, to be a reformer and to lead a movement. Not only was the French influence to be destroyed and the French standards, methods, and tastes to be driven out, but a native taste was to be educated, and true racial forms of

The State Church at Weimar

expression were to be fashioned. Goethe was too self-centered, even in his youth, and of an intellectual fiber too vigorous, to come under the spell of the shallow foreign influence so widely prevalent. The French classicism, which drew its inspiration, not from the originative literature of the Greeks, but from the derivative literature of the Romans, had no charms for a nature so rich in original instincts and so strongly swayed by the free and living forces of the time. It was to the past of his own people that Goethe turned when he wrote, with a strong, vigorous hand, the virile and genuinely German drama of " Götz von Berlichingen "; it was the diseased and disordered fancy among his own Teutonic kin that he portrayed with such searching insight and power in the " Sorrows of Werther." And the storm of acclamation which swept Germany showed how powerfully the chords of racial feeling had been struck and how clear was Goethe's insight into the German nature. It seemed as if a straight and easy road to fame and popularity lay before him; for he had only to hold to Germanic subjects and to the broad, free, Romantic manner to deepen and confirm

149

his hold upon a people who, although become both prosaic and sentimental, had not lost the German feeling, and understood a note struck out of chords long silent, but which had not lost the power of vibration. To Goethe, however, with his extraordinary breadth of view, and his steadily deepening insight into the nature and functions of art, the situation was not so simple; it was, indeed, highly complex. He felt the loneliness of a man superior in gift and vision, not only to his contemporaries, but to his predecessors in his own field. Lessing had much to teach him in the way of clarification of sight; Herder opened up life on all sides by those luminous glances of his into the heart of things; and without the education which he had from Winckelmann he could never have understood Italy and discerned the secret of antique art as he did in the impressionable years of his famous visit. Nevertheless, to a man of Goethe's power, there was the consciousness of creative possibilities as yet unrealized in the native literature, either past or present. If he had been a dramatist by the structure of his mind, there would have been successors to

"Götz" and "Egmont"; but Goethe was a dramatist by intention rather than by nature. He was drawn away, by the immense range of his mind, from the definiteness and concreteness of the dramatic representation of life. He used the dramatic form many times, and with very great success; but, except in the portrayal of two or three women, he does not convey the impression of being compelled to use that form; and in this connection we must recall his own words: "Talent may do what it will; genius does what it must." He could not find expression for the ideas that thronged about in a repetition of his earlier successes. When he came, however, to the question of other and ampler forms of expression, he was confronted by the fact that he must create or introduce them. Neither the German language nor the German literature furnished them ready to his hand. Style in the true sense of the word was almost unknown in Germany. It was not until the publication of "Tasso" that Goethe's own style in its distinction and perfection was discerned; not until the appearance of "Hermann und Dorothea" that the rhythmic possibilities of the German lan-

guage were revealed. Klopstock, Hermann
Grimm tells us, was the creator of modern German prosody; he wrote the first true German
odes, the first real German hexameters; but he
became a mannerist, and he never was, at any
period, a great writer. When " Hermann und
Dorothea " appeared, Gleim declared that the
lovely pastoral was a " sin against his holy
Voss." The famous translation of Homer was
a masterpiece, indeed, and delivered the German hexameter from its academic precision and
artificiality, and gave it the freedom and movement of living speech. It was Goethe, however,
who first touched this verse, so readily made
sluggish and prosaic, with complete ease and
skill, and made it so completely at home in German that it seems the native form of one of the
most charming pastorals in any modern speech.

All this and much more Goethe had to do
to free his own mind and to effect that enlargement of German literature which lay within his
power. " Egmont," " Tasso," " Iphigenia,"
" Faust," were thronging about him in the early
Weimar days; they filled his imagination, but
he seemed incapable of working them out. A

richer atmosphere was necessary; another stage in his development was inevitable. Out of the Germany of 1786, with its poverty of literary art and its defective artistic instinct, Goethe passed into Italy, and came under the full power of that great art to which he had long been drawn, and with which he had so much in common. Then came what has so often been regarded as the break with his past; as if the continuity of a life were to be sought in its works rather than in itself! Whether wisely or unwisely it is unnecessary to discuss here, the writer of the romantic temper and methods became a writer of classical temper and methods. To " Götz " and " Werther " succeeded " Iphigenia," " Tasso," and the " Roman Elegies "; and to the storm of applause which greeted the earlier pieces succeeded the silence of indifference or the murmurs of criticism. Goethe lost his audience, and did not completely regain it until the publication of the first part of " Faust " in 1808. He had not only discarded old forms and employed new ones, but he had wholly changed his attitude toward his work; he not only modeled that work freely on classical

models, but he attempted to detach himself
from it and remove it as definitely from all relation to his life as the works of Sophocles were
freed from all trace of connection, except the
inevitable local color and individual touch, with
the dramatist's personal experience. From
" Iphigenia," " Tasso," the " Roman Elegies,"
and from a number of shorter poems like " The
Bride of Corinth " and " Alexis und Dora,"
Goethe endeavored to detach himself entirely
and to give his work an objectivity as definite
and complete as that of a Greek statue. He did
not succeed, because his works are one and all
rooted in his experience, and because the effort
was out of date; no modern man can do perfectly
what Goethe attempted to do. "Iphigenia" is a
very noble work, but when we search for the essential Goethe we do not look into " Iphigenia "
or " Tasso "; we look into the first part of
" Faust "—the " Faust " of the Romantic, not
the " Faust " of the classical, period. Thus
there appears in the maturity of Goethe's years
and genius a transformation which was regarded at the time and is now regarded by many
as a complete revolution in his aims and meth-

The Castle and Ducal Palace

ods, indeed in his very nature; for it was not
until his return to Weimar, after the two momentous years in Italy, that the charge of coldness began to be heard.

From any point of view, the change is striking and of far-reaching influence, and could
have been possible only in a man to whom his
own country and time did not furnish all the
means of expression he craved, and who was in
the habit of a constant and connected meditation
on his art and his life. A man of Goethe's
years, intelligence, and self-command does not
sever himself from his artistic past, break with
his audience, and essay entirely new methods of
creation without deep and prolonged thought.
Goethe's conversion was rapidly accomplished
in the genial Italian air, but it had been long
in preparation. It is probable that no great
writer ever searched his own nature more rigor-
ously or reflected on the conditions and functions of art more exhaustively than Goethe did
before and after the Italian visit. Every step
away from the earlier standpoint was taken with
deliberate intention and after maturest thought.
The change was the product of a philosophy of

art completely formulated in the poet's mind.
For it is clear that Goethe was drawn away
from the Gothic spirit and the Romantic manner, not by the charm which attaches to the classical form, but by that spell which resides in the
antique view of life and of art as its intimate
and natural expression. Goethe was primarily
an artist, with a lyrical note as clear, personal,
and beguiling as any in literature; art was to
him the one form which life took on that gave
it harmony, unity, and coherence; and he found
in the antique ideals and atmosphere the conditions which made art, not sporadic and individual, but the constant and glorious witness of
the beauty at the heart of all things. If he was
mistaken, there was a noble element in his error;
it was the mistake of an Olympian born in an
age of Titanic unrest and struggle.

In Goethe's nature, moreover, the spontaneous element was always held in check or di-
rected by the rationalizing element. The flowers of song often bloomed very rapidly under
his hand, but in such cases there was always an
antecedent preparation of the soil; the seeds
were already germinating, and the urgence of

some deeply felt experience or the genial
warmth of some prosperous hour or event
swiftly brought the blade to the light.   He
often wrote with great rapidity, but there was
nothing in common between his methods and
the methods of the great improvisers like Byron
and Lope de Vega.   The germinal idea of
" Faust," he tells us, was suddenly unfolded to
his imagination; but he spent sixty years in
working it out!   " The truth is," wrote Lowell
to Mr. Fields, " my brain requires a long brood-
ing-time before it can hatch anything.   As soon
as the life comes into the thing, it is quick
enough in chipping the shell."   With Goethe
the process was not so much brooding over his
theme as looking at it from many sides and putting it into different forms.   During the first
Weimar period, from 1776 to 1786, while he was
so silent and apparently so absorbed in pleasures and administration, " Tasso," " Iphigenia,"
" Egmont," " Wilhelm Meister," and " Faust "
possessed his imagination by turns.   They had
lodged there in those first prodigal years of his
youth at Frankfort.   He not only nourished
and matured them by brooding meditation, but

he gave them shape and form. While " Faust "
and " Wilhelm Meister " received occasional
touches, " Tasso," " Iphigenia," and " Egmont " were written out in forms which were
afterward very largely or wholly discarded.
So far as " Faust " was concerned, it was a kind
of running commentary begun when the poet
was a student and completed in his eighty-sec-
ond year! Evidently, here was a singer whose
gifts were from heaven, but whose methods of
work were as deliberately thought out and his
processes of creation as consciously ordered as
if he had been a child of Mercury rather than
of the Muses. In studying Goethe's genius
one is constantly reminded of the free, spontaneous, and buoyant temper of his mother; in
studying his methods one is reminded of his
precise, orderly, and prosaic father.

There was a distinct vein of philosophic in-
quiry running through Goethe's intellectual
life, and there was a strong critical tendency
in his nature. He was never an orderly thinker,
but he was always striving to arrive at the unity
of things, and to discover those central points
at which the arts and sciences disclosed the iden-

The Bronze Serpent in the Park

tity of their laws and the harmony of their methods. He studied both Spinoza and Kant, not exhaustively, but intelligently; and while he resolutely confined his speculations within the horizons of time and space, he habitually concerned himself with the deeper relations of things, and especially with their relations of interdependence. He cared little for phenomena in themselves, although his attachment to the concrete in nature was so intense as seriously to impair the value of his methods of observation; but he cared greatly for phenomena as they hinted at that interior unity which made them all manifestations of one force. His discovery of the intermaxillary bone and of the typical plant disclose the bent of his mind toward a comprehension of nature as a living whole. In spite of the large place which generalization holds in his work, Goethe was a poet with a philosophic bent rather than a philosopher with a poetic temper. In his old age the didactic mood predominated over the purely artistic, but even in the " Elective Affinities " there are passages of passionate intensity and power.

The critical faculty, when it deals mainly

163

with principles, as in Goethe's case, contains a distinct philosophical element; but its chief characteristic is its power to discern artistic values and to judge artistic processes. It is allied, therefore, with the creative rather than with the purely philosophic mind. Goethe is, on the whole, the greatest of literary critics; indeed, his criticism has such insight and range that he may be called the greatest of art critics. No man has said so many and such luminous things about the artist and the creative mind and mood. A complete philosophy of art, in the widest sense of a much-abused word, lies in his work; a philosophy not like that of Hegel, worked out from the historical standpoint, and with constant reference to its relations with the Absolute; nor like that of Taine, elaborated from the psycho-physiological point of view; but slowly distilled from a prolonged artistic activity, and from first-hand acquaintance with the artistic nature. In this field, as in others, Goethe is fragmentary and defective in logical arrangement; because his conclusions were reached, not as steps in a formal process of thought, but as generaliza-

tions from a growing experience. He does not
discuss art with speculative interest; he speaks
as one having authority, because he discerns
the vital processes and relations of artistic production to the artist and to life. He values
technical skill, and knows the secrets of crafts-
manship; but he is concerned constantly with
art in its fundamental relations with civilization
and with individual experience, and he is in
constant contact with the sources of its power
and freshness. The distinctly judicial activity
of the critical faculty is, nevertheless, always
going on in him, and constantly betrays its presence. So clearly, indeed, does he recognize the
influence of the critical spirit in his own life,
that he has more than once given it objective
form, and Mephistopheles remains the greatest literary representative of the critical spirit
divorced from the creative spirit and become,
therefore, entirely negative and destructive.

There is still another characteristic of Goethe
which must be emphasized in connection with
the rationalizing side of his nature, and that is
the extraordinary intimacy of connection between his works and his experience. All the

greater works of Goethe, even those which, like
" Iphigenia " and " Tasso," seem most detached
from him, were bound up with experiences
through which he had passed, or with persons
whom he had known. The impression, more
than once spread abroad, that he sought the
deeper relations and the more intimate happenings of life for the sake of the literary material
they supplied, is without foundation; it is, indeed, a misrepresentation of a man who, whatever his faults, had a notable kindliness of spirit.
If any criticism is to be made upon Goethe in
this connection, it finds its justification rather
in his studious avoidance of agitating experiences and disturbing relationships; so far was
he from seeking subjects for the kind of vivi-
section which has sometimes been charged
against him. Nor is there a trace of artistic indifference to individual suffering in his dealing
with those relationships of his past in which
others were concerned. What could be more
delicately or tenderly recorded than the idyllic
romance of his student days at Strassburg which
has immortalized Frederika? When this lovely
vision rose before his imagination years after-

The Garden of Goethe's House

ward, his secretary noted the agitation of the old man and the deep silence into which he fell. The disclosure of Goethe's experience in his work has nothing in common with the vulgar invasion of the sanctities of friendship and love of which he has sometimes been accused. There is no record of any light or purely professional use of burned-out passions for the purposes of art. Goethe rationalized his experience and gave it artistic expression from an inward and irresistible impulse; it was the law of his nature, and its necessity as well, to meditate upon everything he had passed through, and to discern in it whatever was beautiful and permanent. No man ever kept a more complete record of his inward life, and outward events found place in that record because they influenced and affected his development. The calmness of his bearing in later years—and it is worth remembering that it is the old Goethe and not the nature or young Goethe whom the world recalls most vividly—cannot hide the tumults and agitations through which he passed, and his imagination kept long in painful touch with experiences which most men would have forgotten. He could rid himself of these haunting memories only by writing them out; when he had given them objective expression, they seemed to detach themselves from him. He did not seek adventures of the heart and the soul; nor did he go about beating the bush for the poetic idea. He was as far as possible removed from the cold, impassive nature turning every emotion to account and following rigidly and haughtily a plan of artistic activity through a long and sedulously guarded life. This is, or has been, the popular ideal of Goethe. It could not have been further from the truth if it had been the popular ideal of Schiller—that eager, restless, aspiring spirit whose life went out in one great breath of aspiration and work.

What strikes one who reads the life of Goethe with insight is his capacity for suffering and his dependence on experience. He had, as an older man, a stiff manner inherited from his father, and he cultivated persistently calmness and repose of spirit because he regarded these qualities as conducive to the ripening of a man's nature, but he was terribly shaken by the sorrows which from time to time knocked at the doors of his strong house. As for his artistic prevision, no great writer was ever more dependent for his material upon what life brought him. He did not forecast his creative activities and give them studied direction; he waited upon life, and he was powerless to create until life, speaking through experience, gave him something to say and the impulse to say it. The work of no other poet reveals a relation so close and constant with the happenings, events, and inward activities of his own history. Beginning with the " Sorrows of Werther," it is possible to connect almost every character in Goethe's books with himself or with some one whom he had known; every incident with some episode in his own story or the story of his friends; almost every experience described or illustrated with some actual experience accessible to him. The history of his loves, his friendships, his journeys, his studies, lies beyond the touch of time in the long record of his dramas, poems, novels, autobiography. His works taken as a whole constitute, as he himself declared, one great confession. Nothing is concealed and very little is extenuated. The truth comes out from beginning to end, and the man's limitations are as evident as his strength. These works fit his vital history like a robe woven of the substance of that which it clothes. Ideas came to him by the way of the heart rather than of the head; and they did not come until he was ripe for them. With all his gifts, he could not have projected into thin air those vast and iridescent dreams of Shelley; he had to keep in constant touch with reality. When he pushed symbolism beyond the limits of his own personal contact with life, as he did in the second part of " Faust," he did not cease to be interesting, but he did cease to be inspired. Among all his beautiful lyrics, unsurpassed in their spontaneity and freshness of feeling and their winged melody, there is barely one which is not known to have risen out of some deep emotion. In works of apparently impersonal character he often speaks most directly out of his heart. In " Tasso " he invests Ferrara with surpassing charm, but he is thinking of Weimar. Every poem and play is a chapter in his biography. He did not seek the materials for artistic activity; they sought him. He did not live for art;

he lived in and through art. Art was his natural
form of expression, and expression was the necessity of his nature, as it is of all rich and
healthy natures. Through this long-sustained
expression there ran a vein of fresh, spontaneous thought and feeling; but so great and
rich a harvest could not have been reaped save
by a deep reflection upon the significance of
these outward happenings. Goethe realized his
experience and made it clear and intelligible
by meditation.

It will be seen, therefore, that the poet's
method of production emphasized the rationalizing tendencies in his nature which have been
indicated, and that the times upon which he was
cast, the natural bent of his mind, his strong
critical instinct, and the dependence of his activity upon his experience, developed and deepened his rationalizing faculty. The crowning
evidence of the influence of the rationalizing
faculty upon his inward life and upon his artistic activity is to be found in the definiteness
of his aims and methods. From a comparatively early period he had determined to make
the most of life by intelligent regulation of his

habits, occupations, and gifts in the interest of complete self-development. Most men take what opportunity offers them and wait on events without understanding them. Goethe resolved to convert all experience into one great opportunity. "From my boyhood," says Wilhelm Meister, "it has been my wish and purpose to develop completely all that is in me, . . . to make my own existence harmonious." In other words, Goethe made a deliberate plan to live his life in his own way and for certain definite ends. "The desire to rear as high as possible in the air the pyramid of my existence, of which the base is given and placed for me, predominates over every other, and scarcely allows itself for a moment to be forgotten." These words, spoken by a man under thirty, were still descriptive of the same man when, at eighty-three, death came to interrupt for the first time habits of work and of thought resolutely pursued for a full half-century. Whatever judgment we may form concerning this plan of life, it is certainly true that it was a plan as deliberately thought out and as resolutely worked out as any of those practical experiments in life by which some of

A Corner in the Garden

the most sincere Greek thinkers evidenced their faith in the reality of philosophy.

From many points of view, therefore, the nature and mind of Goethe disclose the philosophical as distinctly as the creative faculty, the critical as well as the artistic temper, and the rationalizing no less than the spontaneous impulse. In this union of qualities always dissimilar and sometimes antagonistic is found the difficulty of clearly understanding and wisely judging this many-sided man; in this unusual combination is discoverable that element in his work which has made him one of the greatest teachers of all time and one of the foremost intellectual forces of modern times; and in this same combination is to be found the secret of his occasional artistic weakness—a weakness upon which Wordsworth put his hand when he said that Goethe's work is not inevitable enough. Calculation and intention are sometimes in the ascendant, as in the second part of "Faust"; and the spontaneous flow of imagination is neither swift nor deep enough to drain into one current the multitudinous streams which rise over so vast a territory of knowledge and thought.

This rationalizing element runs through all Goethe's work, and gives it a structure of thought of singular massiveness and strength. There is the closest relation between his work and his view or philosophy of life. His artistic impulse, in all his larger work, moved in entire harmony with, and often under the direction of, his rationalizing faculty. He is distinctively the teacher among creative writers; the man who aims not merely at the free expression of his own nature and the creation of beautiful literary forms, but also at definite exposition, through the medium of art, of certain general views. This could hardly have been otherwise in one who held so serious a view of art, and to whom it was of such supreme importance as the final expression of the mind and heart of man. For with Goethe, as with all the greater artists, life is primary and art secondary in the order of time; but both are parts of one complete expression of the soul. In Goethe's case, however, this process of thought is more definitely marked than in the case of any of his peers; and it was probably more self-conscious and self-directed.

The Valley of the Doones

THE LAND OF LORNA DOONE

THE LAND OF LORNA DOONE

HE artistic value of backgrounds is strikingly shown in Mr. Blackmore's one successful novel, "Lorna Doone." There are other stories of his which are not without charming qualities, but on this romance alone has he put the stamp of beauty and individuality. "Lorna Doone" cannot be regarded as a great story; it is, rather, a lovable story—one of those pieces of art that live by reason of their close touch upon the most intimate and tender of human relations; a story which, upon analysis, reveals serious faults of construction and defects of style, but which nobody is willing to analyze. It is too long; it

drags in places; the manner, under the guise of great simplicity, is sometimes artificial; and yet it captivates, and its charm is likely to abide.

That charm resides in two elements—its idyllic love story, and its impressive background. If the drama of John Ridd and Lorna Doone had been played on a commonplace stage, it could hardly have appealed with such beguiling force to the imagination; it is because through it, as through an open window, we are always looking out on the wild, romantic Valley of the Doones that it lives in memory and recalls us to many a quiet re-reading. To a Devonshire man, as Blackmore reports with evident satisfaction, " Lorna Doone " is " as good as clotted cream," that delicious product of the dairies of Devon. It is redolent of Devon and Somerset, two counties which in variety and richness of scenery must be ranked among the first in England. John Ridd belonged to both counties, and both have given the story the charm of landscapes of noble breadth and ripest beauty.

There is no better approach to the Valley of the Doones than a drive across country from

THE LAND OF LORNA DOONE

Bideford. At nightfall, in that quaint old town, one may look across the Torridge and see the lights shining from the low windows of "The Ship Tavern," where Salvation Yeo and his fellows once talked far into the night of the perils of the Spanish Main. One may, if he chooses, sit in the room in which much of the work of preparation for the writing of "Westward Ho" was done. On a soft summer morning, the low sky veiled with a pale mist, no road could be more beguiling than that which takes one from the old seaport, where famous sailors were bred in the sixteenth century, into the heart of the lovely Devonshire landscape, with its bold lines of hills, its rich verdure, its fields ripe with the deep-rooted loveliness of ancient fertility, its hedges so high that one is often shut in between impenetrable walls of hawthorn and privet.

For hours through this quiet world of old-time beauty one drives in absolute solitude; not even a cart comes down the long hills or around the winding curves of the road. Later, as one nears Lynton, coaches will thunder past; but across country this western corner of England

is as quiet as it was in the days before tele-
phones vexed the ear with the noise of distant
cities. In some corner of a field or some bend
in the road, under immemorial oaks or beeches,
there is fitting time for luncheon and a quiet
nooning for the horses. If there happens to be
a long hill ahead, one walks on in advance, stopping now and again to enter some newly har-
vested field and catch another glimpse of the
fertile landscape where long service of human
needs has bred a deep sense of fellowship between man and meadow. In one of these little
incursions one may meet a typical English
farmer, taking time for a turn with his pipe and
predisposed to friendly talk, with a vein of
characteristic criticism of the Government, the
state of agriculture, and the English system in
general; for farmers are much the same the
world over, and are rarely without good-hu-
mored grievances against existing conditions.

At the end of the afternoon the landscape
changes, and one comes out upon Exmoor, with
its broad expanse of gently sloping moor,
brown or green, with touches of purple bell-
heather. The noble coast lies but a mile or two

beyond; and there again the landscape changes, and the cliffs of Devon stand in the sea, rocky and castellated or green to the very edges where the tides rise and fall.

It is a noble approach which one makes who goes to the Valley of the Doones from Lynton; at once wild, solitary, and beautiful with the loveliness of color, of moving streams, and of bold hillsides. There are passes between the hills so deep and densely overhung with trees that it is easy to imagine the sudden descent of the robber band from the hills, the brief struggle, and the swift success of the adventure. Below the road runs the stream which is fed by the two brooks which flow together at Watersmeet. The meeting of these mountain brooks is a place of rare beauty, where Bryant would have found the charm of solitude which laid its spell upon him in Flora's Glen among the Berkshires, with an added wildness of hill and an added loveliness of ancient water flowing through moss-grown beds. There is a choice of roads, and the well-informed go in by one route and return by another. The road through the valley of the Brendon runs through the quaint hamlet which bears the name of the stream; the little villages are much alike: a church, a parsonage, a few laborers' houses, a small inn, and sometimes a picturesque house of size, solidity, and an air of assured position.

The little hamlet of Oare is one of the focal points in the story, and there still stands the old church in which Lorna and John were married, where the true-hearted girl fell into the arms of the faithful lover, and from which John rushed in a mad passion and heartbreak to settle the long score with Carver Doone. It is a tiny building, well hidden by trees, with a low square tower, a nave so small that it seems like a toy structure, and a chancel as tiny; one of those quaint little churches which one finds in England, with room for but a handful of people, but touched with old associations and giving a quiet landscape a hint of ancient worship and half-forgotten history. In this church John Ridd held office as warden with a deep sense of his unfitness.

The Plover's Barrows Farm of John Ridd's time has vanished, but its site is pointed out, and one needs no imagination to look upon the landscape through his eyes: " Almost everybody knows, in our part of the world at least, how pleasant and soft the fall of the land is round Plover's Barrows Farm. Above it is strong dark mountains, spread with heath, and desolate, but near our house the valleys cove, and open warmth and shelter. Here are trees, and bright green grass, and orchards full of contentment, and a man scarce espy the brook, although he hears it everywhere, and, indeed, a stout good piece of it comes through our farmyard, and swells sometimes to a rush of waves, when the clouds are on the hilltops. But all below, where the valley bends, and the Lyn stream goes along with it, pretty meadows slope their breast, and the sun spreads on the water." Here lived the Ridds—slow-witted, big-framed, honest-hearted farmer folk; loving the soil which they had worked for generations; clean-handed, God-fearing men and women of the stock which has given England an immovable foundation.

The Bagsworthy Valley lies a mile or more beyond, and here, at Bagsworthy Farm, one leaves the road and follows a footpath along the

189

stream for three miles, through the haunts and home of the Doones. It is a beautiful glen, with a certain wildness and brooding desolation quite in keeping with its associations; but it is less bold and its sides are less precipitous than the descriptions in " Lorna Doone " suggest. The hillsides are steep and barren save for the bell-heather which softens their outlines, and the narrow valley has an atmosphere of remoteness and desolation. The waterslide, when it is reached, seems much less alarming than it appeared to John Ridd when he made his perilous ascent; and the Doone Gate is a rocky mound which is easily accessible.

It must not be forgotten that John Ridd's imagination was filled for years with an almost superstitious dread of the Doones, whose recklessness, audacity, quick intelligence, and long defiance of law had deeply impressed the whole countryside with a sense of terror, so that the Doone Valley became an accursed place, full of all manner of known or unimaginable terrors. Moreover, it is more than two centuries since the spell of the Doones was broken and their nest burned over their heads, and every year in that long period has softened and subdued their old haunt. The Exmoor of to-day is a very different landscape from that upon which men looked in the time when Judge Jeffreys was holding the " bloody assizes." A century later Exmoor was " a land of freedom and solitude, haunt of the bittern and red deer, intersected by many a silent tomb and brawling river." The red deer are still there, and the wild, lonely beauty of the heaths and of the Valley of the Doones is untouched; but Mother Melldrum no longer hides in the Valley of the Rocks, the old superstitions have become pleasant legends for the entertainment of tourists, the Doones have ceased to be terrible and become romantic, and their valley has exchanged its inaccessible savagery for a wild loveliness which is somewhat secluded but quite within reach of the pedestrian. In the novel we see through John Ridd's eyes; and, honest and literal as the slow-thinking but stout-hearted lover of Lorna was, his imagination was not untouched by the wild tales and superstitious fears of his time.

Coming out of this lonely valley, with its

tragic legend of ancient wrong rudely avenged, and its tender story of old-time love transmuted into lifelong happiness, one is prepared for the noble drive across the summits of the hills, splendid beyond words with the purple of the bell-heather, mile upon mile of unbroken color against the sky, with long contrasts of yellow gorse; the great cliffs green or bare to the water, and the sea softly blue in the long summer twilight; a noble country, molded on large lines, with a richness of verdure which has its roots in unnumbered centuries; lonely heaths, great hills shouldering one another to the line of the sky, and a valley sacred to the memory of a beautiful romance and of a novelist who touched the heart of his generation.

Whitman's Birthplace

AMERICA IN WHITMAN'S POETRY

AMERICA IN WHITMAN'S POETRY

T the funeral of William
Cullen Bryant the most con-
spicuous figure was Walt
Whitman. Far apart as the
two men were in educa-
tion, association, ideas, and
methods of art, there was one
striking resemblance between them: they were
both elemental poets dealing with a few fundamental things. Bryant's range was narrow,
but the vastness of nature in the New World
came into view for the first time in his verse;
and what he lacked in breadth was supplied, in
part at least, by his altitude of thought. In
Whitman's verse, on the other hand, the sense
of space is pervasive; it is all out-of-doors; from

every point the horizons are visible. One misses the heights of spiritual vision, the power and joy in moral achievement; but one feels the presence, in an original and powerful way, of the most inclusive human sympathy, the most sincere human fellowship.

In the same year Whitman spoke on Lincoln to a small audience in a New York theater, made up largely of men and women interested in literature. The poet was then in his sixtieth year, but looked much older: a large, impressive figure, lacking muscular force and conveying no impression of physical strength, but massive, benignant, with a certain dignity of bulk and carriage. A gray suit, carelessly worn but admirably harmonized with the head and frame, suggested that the poet had not wholly lost the self-consciousness with which he began his career as the founder of a new school of song. His face was large, kindly, and warmly tinted; his head nobly set off by flowing white hair; his bearing toward his audience free, cordial, and unaffected. He read his prose as he wrote it, with frequent parentheses, pauses, asides, excursions into neighboring subjects; but his manner had flavor, individuality, native quality. At the close he recited " O Captain! My Captain!" with such simplicity and depth of feeling that his audience felt that they were hearing the noblest man of the heroic age celebrated by its most rugged and powerful bard.

The appearance of Whitman, the shape of his head, the detachment of his life, the dithyrambic quality of his verse and its irregular and uncertain flow, the richness of his lyrical impulse and the uncertainty of his judgment, the broad, elemental conception of life and art which he held—all these things suggest the bard, the rhapsodical singer of a simple society and an objective age, rather than the many-sided interpreter in song of the rich complexity of modern life. A primitive person Whitman was in many ways; and he shared with the skalds, bards, and prophets of earlier and less sophisticated races much of their affluence and spontaneity of expression, their rejection of the subtleties and refinements of art; but he was in more respects the most modern of poets. In his conception of society, of the place and dignity of the individual, of the worth and beauty of the body and all its functions, in his use of forms of poetic expression, in his hearty acceptance of science, he marks the extreme reaction against the classical, the mediæval, the aristocratic, the æsthetic ideals of the past.

In his rejection of the accepted verse-forms he imagined himself creating a new poetic language vitally adapted to the expression of a new poetic thought; while, as a matter of fact, he was reviving and remodeling some of the oldest verse-forms. No man, however radical in instinct and intention, ever really breaks away from his race and creates new things out of hand. The race is far greater in its collective genius and experience than any individual member, and the most original man must be content to give some ancient divination a clearer statement, to touch some old experience with fresh feeling, to open a vista, to set the feet of men again on a path which their fathers once trod, but which they left for some other and more inviting road. Whitman revives, in his underlying thought, one of the oldest Oriental conceptions of the order and significance of life; in his verse-forms he restores and gives contemporary currency to ancient methods of versification. These elements in his work, which were loudly acclaimed as novel, are of a hoary antiquity; what is new and significant in him is his resolute acceptance of the democratic order in all its logical sequences, his instinctive and sane feeling that if great poetry is to be written on this continent it must find its themes, not in the interests of the few, but in the occupation and experience of the many; above all, he brought to his work a vital, searching, pictorial imagination of great compass and power of illumination.

There is much that is repellent in his work; much that is coarse, gross, offensively and pedantically lacking in reticence, in regard for the sanctities of the body and of the relations between men and women, which the ascetic and the sensualist have alike misunderstood and misinterpreted. There is much in his egotism, his aggressive and ill-timed assertion of himself; there has been much, too, in the ill-advised and unintelligent advocacy of some of his devotees, that have combined to keep sane readers at a distance. These advocates have too often taken the attitude toward other American poets that

some missionaries have taken toward the gods
of the countries in which they have taught a new
faith; they have sent them all to perdition together. Students of literary history are too
familiar with mutations of taste to be affected
by the claims of exclusive originality in any
poet. They are not disturbed about the security
of Shakespeare and Milton, and they are at
ease about the survival of Emerson and Poe.
They are ready to accept the new, but they do
not intend to reject the old; for the old that
survives is always new. They have seen the ir-
ruptions of the barbarians before, and have
heard the crash of the falling gods; and they
have lived to see the destroyers not only replac-
ing the gods, but striving with pathetic eagerness to recall the vanished skill which long ago
imparted the touch of divinity. The new artist
succeeds by the new illustration of that creative
power which bears in every age immortal fruit.
If Whitman is to be accepted as a poetic force
of high authority, it will not be by dethroning
his predecessors, but by establishing his right to
reign with them.

The real contribution made by Whitman to

Old Well at Huntington

American literature is the marvelously vivid
picture of a democratic society in its workaday
aspects, its primal and basal instincts, emotions,
occupations. In a very real, though not in an
exclusive or ultimate, sense he is the poet of democracy; that, as Professor Dowden and other
discerning critics beyond the sea saw when his
work first came into their hands, is his fundamental significance, his original quality. In
his case, therefore, the background of his poetry
is one of its formative elements; it furnished the
material with which he worked.

That man is fortunately born the conditions
of whose early life put him and keep him in intimate and vital relation with the kind of experience, the social habits and circumstances,
with which he is later to deal with original insight and power. Whitman was born in a
place that gave easy access to open fields, to the
sea, and to great cities, and in a condition that
brought him into contact with working America.
He and Lanier are the only American poets of
high rank who have been born out of New England; and there is in them both a quality of imagination which no other American poets pos-

sess. In neither was there that balance between inspiration and achievement, that equality of insight with expression, which the greatest singers possess, but both disclosed an affluent and plastic imagination of a new order in this country. Two men could hardly have been further apart in education, ideal, character; but they are the two great figures in the opening of the National period which followed the close of the Civil War; and a century hence, when American literature shall have struck deep into the almost unexplored depths of American life, their significance will be very great.

Whitman was born at West Hills, Long Island, on May 31, 1819. Dutch and English blood was in his veins, and he was the child of working people, farmers, mechanics; men and women who used their hands as well as their brains. On the father's side there was a strain of sluggishness in the blood, but with latent impetuosity and vehemence of feeling and action on occasion. The Quaker tradition had ceased to affect the dress and speech of the family, but it bore its fruit in a fundamental faith in individual guidance and in a free but reverential attitude toward religion.

AMERICA IN WHITMAN'S POETRY

The elder Whitman had been a carpenter, but during his residence in West Hills was a builder of excellent reputation for skill and thoroughness. The poet's mother was a large, quiet, strong woman, with little education, but of a deep nature; " benignant, calm, practical, spiritual " are the adjectives with which her son described her. The house in which Walt Whitman was born, which is still standing, was already a century old at his birth, and the farm had been in possession of the family for three generations—a period long enough, as these things are reckoned in England, to make a " county family."

" The Whitmans, at the beginning of the present century," writes Mr. Burroughs, " lived in a long, story-and-a-half farm-house, hugely timbered, which is still standing. A great smoke-canopied kitchen, with vast hearth and chimney, formed one end of the house. The existence of slavery in New York at that time, and the possession by the family of some twelve or fifteen slaves, house and field servants, gave things quite a patriarchal look. The very young darkies could be seen, a swarm of them, toward sundown, in this kitchen, squatted in a circle on the floor, eating their supper of Indian pudding and milk. In the house, and in food and furniture, all was rude but substantial. No carpets or stoves were known, and no coffee and tea, and sugar only for the women. Rousing wood fires gave both warmth and light on winter nights. Pork, poultry, beef, and all the ordinary vegetables and grains were plentiful. Cider was the men's common drink, and used at meals. The clothes were mainly homespun. Journeys were made by both men and women on horseback. Both sexes labored with their own hands—the men on the farm, the women in the house and around it. Books were scarce. The annual copy of the almanac was a treat, and was pored over through the long winter evenings. I must not forget to mention that both these families were near enough to the sea to behold it from the high places, and to hear in still hours the roar of the surf; the latter, after a storm, giving a peculiar sound at night. Then all hands, male and female, went down frequently on beach and bathing parties, and the men on practical expeditions for cutting salt hay, and for clamming and fishing."

AMERICA IN WHITMAN'S POETRY

A county family in the English sense the
Whitmans were not; but they had stayed long
enough in one place, and been long enough engaged in work, to take root in the soil and to
disclose the influence of long-continued tasks on
a succession of workers. The Whitmans were
large, plain, simple people, who possessed the
elemental things of life and cared for little else;
they showed no marked intellectual aptitudes;
no passion for education appeared in any generation; they were industrious, capable working
people, curiously devoid, it would seem, of the
American ambition to " get on " in life.

As a boy at West Hills, and later in Brooklyn, Walt Whitman showed the out-of-doors
habit that was characteristic of the family, and
spent many profitable days not only in explor-
ing the western end of Long Island from the
Sound to the ocean, but in letting the atmosphere of the woods and fields envelop and color
his imagination. He was then, as later, a loi-
terer; a habit of mind and body that made him
not only tolerant of " loafers," but disposed to
regard " loafing " as a dignified occupation.
The trouble with most " loafing " is that it is

unaccompanied with an invitation to the soul,
to recall Whitman's phrase, to be at ease in
the world and share its growth while the body
is quiescent.

There was some attendance on the public
schools, but at thirteen the future poet went
into a lawyer's office; then turned his attention
to medicine; became a printer; taught country
schools; wrote for the country newspapers; established a journal of his own; passed the years
from 1840 to 1845 in New York as a compositor
in printing-offices, spending his summers in the
country and working on the farm; writing essays and tales. In 1842 he published " Frank-
lin Evans; or, The Inebriate: A Tale of the
Times," dedicated to the Temperance Societies.
This story has, fortunately, disappeared; its
chief characteristics, according to the report of
two of the poet's biographers, were " its flam-
boyant phrase " and " its puritan odor of sanctity." Whitman's later work did not entirely
escape the first of these qualities; of the second
not a trace remained. This stage of his life
closed with two years of editorial work on the
Brooklyn "Eagle." In 1848, in his thirtieth

year, he made a long journey through the Middle, Southern, and Western States, ending with a visit of some length in New Orleans, where he became intensely interested in the picturesque and significant aspects of Southern life. He returned to Brooklyn and to journalism, and finally engaged for a time in building and selling houses in that city. In 1855 " Leaves of Grass " appeared, and his life entered on an entirely different stage.

The years at West Hills, in Brooklyn and New York, and the time given to travel, constitute the educational period in Whitman's life; and while he was entirely familiar with some great formative books and deeply influenced by them, he was trained for his work out-of-doors. Few men have known so many kinds of people and been so much at home with men simply as men. Whitman had a passion for humanity, without reference to character, education, occupation, condition. The streets, ferry-boats, tops of stages, loafing-places, were dear to him because they gave him a chance to see men and women in the whole range of the conditions and accidents of life.

He drew no lines and made no distinctions; the saint and the sinner, the nun and the prostitute, the hero and the criminal, were alike to him in their fundamental appeal to his interest. He went to the churches, the great reform meetings, the best theaters; and he went also to hospitals, poorhouses, prisons. He had friends among cultivated people, but he loved the native qualities of humanity, and was most at home with working people—pilots, masons, teamsters, deck-hands, mechanics of all sorts; men who toil, as his ancestors had toiled, with the hands. He went wherever people were to be found, and spent a great deal of time in the streets and at popular resorts of every kind. "He made himself familiar with all kinds of employments," writes Dr. Bucke, " not by reading trade reports and statistics, but by watching and stopping hours with the workmen (often his intimate friends) at their work. He visited the foundries, shops, rolling-mills, slaughter-houses, woolen and cotton factories, ship-yards, wharves, and the big carriage and cabinet shops; went to clam-bakes, races, auctions, weddings, sailing and bathing parties, christenings, and all kinds of merrymakings. He knew every New York omnibus-driver, and found them both good comrades and capital materials for study. Indeed, he tells us that the influence of these rough, good-hearted fellows (like the Broadway stage-driver in ' To Think of Time ') undoubtedly entered into the gestation of ' Leaves of Grass.' No scene of natural beauty, no ' apple-tree blows of white and pink in the orchard,' no lilac-bush ' with every leaf a miracle,' no ' gorgeous, indolent, sinking sun, burning, expanding the air,' no ' hurrying-tumbling waves,' no ' healthy uplands, with herby-perfumed breezes,' give him greater inspiration than the thronged streets of New York, with the ' interminable eyes,' with the life of the theater, barroom, huge hotel, the saloon of the steamer, the crowded excursion, ' Manhattan crowds, with their turbulent musical chorus,' the rushing torrent, the never-ceasing roar, of modern human life." He was no stranger, however, in libraries and museums, and his walks afield were long and fruitful. With his knapsack, a bit of luncheon, a copy of Shakespeare or Homer, he spent long solitary days on the sea-shore, often reciting aloud like the older bards whose lineal descendant he was. He was sensitive to music, and the opera gave him unqualified delight. He described the once famous contralto Alboni as " the blooming mother, sister of loftiest Gods." He knew Wagner's music only by report, but that he divined something of its significance is evident from his remark: " I know from the way you fellows talk of it that the music of Wagner is the music of the ' Leaves.' "

So far Whitman had seen life chiefly and by choice in its fundamental occupations, its simplest aspects; he was now to see it on the tragic side, and to be profoundly touched and influenced by it. In the second year of the Civil War he went to Washington and became a volunteer nurse in the army hospitals, supporting himself by writing letters to the New York " Times." At the close of the war he became a clerk in the Interior Department, a position from which he was unwisely removed because of certain passages in the " Leaves of Grass." Later he obtained a place in the Treasury Department, which he retained until 1873, when he was partially disabled by a slight stroke of paralysis. In the spring of that year he removed to Camden, N. J., where he had a modest home and saw many friends. His means were very limited, but they were supplemented by the devotion of his friends. His health was much impaired, but his cheerfulness was unclouded. There, on the 26th of March, 1892, he died, and lies buried in a Camden cemetery.

Against the background of childhood, youth, and the years of active and of reflective life, sketched in the simplest lines, Whitman stands out with great distinctness and in striking contrast with his peers among American men of letters. With one exception, they were university-bred men, born into the gentlest and best social traditions, within reach of the ripest intellectual influences, in touch with the finest expressions of the human spirit in its long historic unfolding. Whitman's heritage was of a different kind; the influences which touched him immediately and most powerfully issued out of contemporaneous life; he knew a few books well, and they were among the greatest—the Bible, Homer in translation, Shakespeare, Don Quixote; he read Hegel, Tennyson, Emerson, Carlyle, and other typical modern writers; but he found his material and his inspiration in the America which he saw with his eyes, touched with his hand, and divined with his heart—the America of active life, of colossal energy, of native manliness, of free, unconventional, friendly living. This America of the farm, the workshop, the railroad, the prairie, the mining camp, the rushing, tumultuous play of elemental forces, he saw with a clearness of vision that no other poet has possessed, and described with a freshness and boldness of phrase that give incontrovertible evidence of real poetic power. This physical and social America is the background of his poetry; and in making it his background Whitman struck his one original note and made his one contribution to our literature.

An English critic has said recently of William Morris that, passionate as was his reaction against the ugliness of contemporary life and his determination to bring the beautiful back to its old place and function, his inability to turn a personal conviction into an overwhelming movement was evidenced by his failure to give

The Garden of Whitman's House in Camden

common, modern, useful things beautiful forms. He could give a chest or chair or table the exquisite symmetry or the massive lines which they had in their best estate, but he did not give us artistic lamp-posts and letter-boxes. Whitman did precisely this; he took the roughest material close at hand, and not only divined its poetic significance, but resolutely set himself the task of making others recognize it. He was, fortunately, so accustomed to uncouthness, roughness, crudity, that these early conditions of all vital things did not repel him; on the contrary, they appealed to his imagination. He had grown up with them and made friends with them in those sensitive hours when the imagination forms its intimacies; and the great rough, crude life of the new continent opened its heart to him. Other poets had divined what was in the American spirit and had heard notes that escaped him, but Whitman was the first poet to get into his verse the continental volume of American life, its vast flow through the channels of a thousand occupations, its passionate practice of equality, its resolute assertion of the sanctity of the individual, its insistence on the supreme value of the native as against the acquired traits and qualities.

That Whitman lost perspective and blurred the scale of values by breaking even partially with the long line of those who, in the days before him, had seen life at first hand is clear enough; but it may have been necessary for some poet to take democracy in its most elementary form, without shading or qualification, to clear the way for the greater poet who will some day speak out of a knowledge as searching, a sympathy as profound, but with a clearer discernment of spiritual degrees and orders. Whitman did what no other poet had done: he accepted not only the democratic ideal, but the life organized under it, without qualification, and with a deep joy in the new disclosure of the human spirit, the fresh evocation of human energy, which it effected. Here and now, he declared, the American poet must claim his hour and his material; in the meanest and the worst the soul of goodness survives, in the roughest and crudest the soul of beauty hides itself. Some of that goodness he evoked, some of that beauty he made manifest. His attitude is expressed in lines which are prosaic in form but which reveal his point of view and suggest the sources of his inspiration:

I hear America singing, the varied carols I hear,
Those of mechanics, each one singing his as it should
    be blithe and strong;
The carpenter singing his as he measures his plank
    or beam,
The mason singing his as he makes ready for work, or
    leaves off work,
The boatman singing what belongs to him in his
    boat, the deck-hand singing on the steamboat deck,
The shoemaker singing as he sits on his bench, the hatter
    singing as he stands,
The wood-cutter's song, the ploughboy's on his way in
    the morning, or at noon intermission or at sundown,
The delicious singing of the mother, or of the young
    wife at work, or of the girl sewing or washing,
Each singing what belongs to him or her and to none
    else,
The day what belongs to the day—at night the party
    of young fellows, robust, friendly,
Singing with open mouths their strong melodious songs.

Emerson expressed the American spirit with singular clarity and beauty of phrase; Whitman expressed the volume and range of American life; the greater poet who is to come will compass both spirit and body. He will honor man as man, labor as labor, the common use because it is common, as Whitman honored these things; he will exalt the basal elements; but he will not rest in these primary stages of growth; he will not set the man in his undeveloped strength in antagonism with the man in his trained and ordered maturity.

The mistake which many Whitman devotees have made is an old and familiar one; they have set the crude man in antagonism to the developed man; they have decried refinement, delicacy, sensitiveness, as signs of weakness and exalted the elementary forms of power as the only kinds of power. The cowboy and the miner are picturesque figures, but the force they represent is not a whit more normal and is far less highly organized than that of countless intrepid, accomplished men who are carrying the burdens of society and doing its work in all departments without publicity or craving for applause. We need to get back to the primitive qualities from time to time, and it is a suggestive fact that, as a rule, it is those who are overtrained on some side who are clamorous for a return to primitive types and modes. But nature does not rest in these lower types; she steadily perfects her types by development. In the reaction against the conventional, artificial, purely academic view of things, it is sometimes necessary to break a few windows; but breaking windows is always a temporary measure. Culture in the true sense is simply the process of growth, and the man who fulfils his life by unfolding all his powers is a more natural man than he who has suffered an arrest of his development. Democracy cannot change the laws which govern human life; it will be a great gain if it can bring in simplicity of living; it is quite certain that it cannot and ought not to preserve native flavor by retarding normal growth. American literature will never become powerful by the exaltation of the rough, the crude, the unclean; what it lacks is not frankness, but the original power which pierces to the heart of society and lays bare its dramatic significance as Thackeray did in "Vanity Fair." Great writers do not need to be either profane or obscene.

Whitman was a pathfinder, and his joy in the

223

great new world of human experience that he explored no one would take from him. It will be seen some day that there was a true prophetic strain in him, and that he marked the beginning, not of a new kind of literature, but of a new and National stage of literary development in this country. In his verse the sections disappear and the Nation comes into view, the provinces fade and the continent defines itself. It is man at work over a continent that stirs him; he celebrates few persons; Lincoln alone seems to have moved him profoundly; even when he celebrates himself it is as a kind of incarnation and embodiment of human qualities and experiences. In this attitude he was instinctively expressing his conception of Democracy as a vast brotherhood, in which all men are on an equality, irrespective of individual traits and qualities.

There is nothing finer in Whitman than his passion for comradeship; in his idealization of the fellowship between man and man he not only sounded some great, sincere notes, but he struck out some great lines in the heat of a feeling which seems always to have had quick access to his imagination. To this all-embracing affection, so deeply rooted in his conception of the democratic order, he devotes a large group of poems under the title " Calamus." These friends of the spirit are not chosen by any principle of taste; they are chiefly " powerful uneducated persons ":

I am enamour'd of growing out-doors,
Of men that live among cattle or taste of the ocean or
    woods,
Of the builders and steerers of ships and the wielders of
    axes and mauls, and the drivers of horses,
I can eat and sleep with them week in and week out.

It cannot be said with justice that Whitman erases all moral distinctions and rejects entirely the scale of spiritual values; but it is quite certain that he blurs them, and reduces his world to unity by putting aside resolutely the principle of selection. His underlying religious conception of life is essentially Oriental, and dates back to the time before the idea of personality had been clearly grasped. This principle Whitman does not consistently apply, for he lays tremendous emphasis on " powerful uneducated persons "; but in a certain sense it is wrought into his presentation of the democratic society.

225

In that presentation individuals sink into the vast community whose naked energy, power, vigor, and habit the poet loves to paint. Neither in life nor in art, in the material which he uses nor in the form in which he casts it, does he employ that skill in selection which is one of the prime gifts of the artist. Whitman shows, as a consequence, no power of self-criticism; no ability to distinguish the good from the bad in his work, to separate poetry from prose. He has left a few pieces of unique quality of imagination and harmony embedded in a great mass of unorganized poetic material. In reading him one feels as if he were going through a vast atelier crowded with blocks of unhewn marble and huge piles of débris, with here and there a statue of noble and even majestic proportions. Whitman is easily travestied, but no one has ever done this impious thing half so well as he did himself in some of his most pretentious pieces. His devotees would render him the truest service if they would stop chanting his praise and thoroughly and critically edit his works.

Whitman's great gift is his imagination, which is deep, fervent, pictorial, penetrating;

At Cold Spring Harbor, where Whitman had his First Glimpse of the Sea

an imagination, in force, volume, and power of
flooding a great theme, quite beyond anything
in our literature. In the New England poets
generally the thinking faculty is more powerful
than the faculty which makes images; this is
the limitation of our earlier poets. There is too
much intellect, which analyzes, separates, and
defines, and too little imagination, which fuses,
combines, and personifies. At his best, Whitman's imagination has a tidal movement and
depth. When " Out of the Cradle Endlessly
Rocking " is read, with that intelligence of feeling which keeps the thought and tune in unison
and makes them mutually interpretative, the
sensitive listener is aware of a power which lies
deeper than that put forth by any other American poet, and which has an elemental energy
and sweep; as if nature had conspired with the
poet and given his song a touch of her mystery and the ultimate music of those secret processes which build, out of sight, the beauty of
the world. In such poems as " The Mystic
Trumpeter," the " Passage to India," " When
Lilacs Last in the Dooryard Bloom'd," " Out
of the Cradle Endlessly Rocking," " O Cap-

tain! My Captain!" Whitman establishes himself, not only among the first of our poets, but, in respect of imaginative power, the first of the goodly company. This free and noble use of the creative faculty, at once unconventional and obedient to the law of art, is revealed in such lines as these:

Here are our thoughts, voyager's thoughts,
Here not the land, firm land, alone appears, may then
by them be said,
The sky o'erarches here, we feel the undulating deck beneath our feet,
We feel the long pulsation, ebb and flow of endless motion,
"he tones of unseen mystery, the vague and vast suggestions of the briny world, the liquid-flowing syllables,
The perfume, the faint creaking of the cordage, the melancholy rhythm,
The boundless vista and the horizon far and dim are all here,
And this is ocean's poem.

Such passages as this, vital, fresh, deeply suggestive, full of the eternal movement of things, show the elemental power of this extraordinary man to whom nature gave so much; but this great gift was beset with marked limitations, and the spring of pure song often gushes out in a dreary waste of long-drawn-out categories and vast stretches of barren prose.

Whitman, like Wordsworth, took himself at all times as one inspired; but with him, as with the author of the Ecclesiastical Sonnets, there were long periods of uninspired dullness. And there is no conformity so monotonous as that of the nonconformist. Whitman's irregular dithyrambic verse is immensely impressive when the full tide of his imagination floods it, but when that tide is out it becomes machinery of the most ponderous kind. Much has been said about this verse as something new in the world; as a matter of fact, it belongs to very ancient poetry. That diminishes not a whit the greatness of Whitman's achievement, but it keeps us to the fact, which is quite essential in any adequate judgment of a man's work. Much has been said also about this verse as belonging to nature rather than to art; as if art were something other than the best and therefore the most natural way of doing a thing. And so sound a critic as Mr. Burroughs has spoken, in this connection, of Tennyson and Browning as " literary poets "; implying, apparently, that Whitman was of a different kind. Now, in so far as Whitman was a poet he was a literary poet; when he is at his best his verse conforms to certain laws of art as truly as the verse of the great poets who went before him. When he ceases to be literary in this sense, he ceases to be interesting. Nature and art are never antagonistic; they are supplementary. Whitman did not react against art, but against artifice, which is a very different matter. That Whitman had the feeling for art, for that order which reveals without intruding the most vital relations, is evident not only in his work at its best, but in his strikingly effective arrangement of his verse and prose in the forms in which he finally gave them to the world.

No one has defined more impressively than Whitman the quality in writing which gives it that life that is always synonymous with the highest art:

" The art of art, the glory of expression and the sunshine of the light of letters is simplicity. Nothing is better than simplicity . . . nothing can make up for excess or for the lack of definiteness. To carry on the heave of impulse and pierce intellectual depths and give all subjects their articulations are powers neither common nor very uncommon. But to speak in literature with the perfect rectitude and insouciance of the movements of animals and the unimpeachableness of the sentiment of trees in the woods and grass by the roadside is the flawless triumph of art. If you have looked on him who has achieved it you have looked on one of the masters of the artists of all nations and times."

Nothing could be more just and penetrating than this definition of the quality of a great writer; by this definition Whitman's work must be tried; applying this test to that work, it appears that some of it will survive and much of it will be cast aside. The race is already too heavily encumbered with luggage of all sorts; all the great writers must submit to a rigid re-examination from time to time; and Whitman will not be exempt from a test which has been applied to Goethe, to Wordsworth, and to Byron. And it may be suspected that Whitman succeeds greatly where he conforms most closely to the great tradition of art which is the faithful

and devout practice of all the great poets, and
that he fails most lamentably where he attempts
deliberately to create a new method. It is quite
certain that in his case, as in that of Browning,
the devotees have exalted his eccentricities and
belittled his sanest and truest work. A man of
original force like Whitman has far more to
fear from injudicious and uncritical friends
than from scornful and unsympathetic enemies.

In his exaltation of the body Whitman's
thought is less gross than his speech; and at his
worst his coarse frankness is more wholesome
than the subtle and less offensive but far more
corrupt treatment of such themes by some of
the contemporary writers of the decadent school.
Compared with the exquisitely artistic corruption which D'Annunzio analyzes and depicts
with such searching insight, Whitman's nudity
of image and phrase is health itself. The ob-
jection to Whitman's handling of these delicate
and profoundly significant relations is not that
it is unclean, but that it is inartistic. It is not
immoral in the sense that it is corrupt, but it is
immoral because it violates that instinct of reticence which protects these relations by keeping

fresh the sentiment which invests them with the poetry of the creative process. This poetry Whitman ruthlessly destroys by denuding the whole mysterious relation of its mystery. In nothing does he more clearly reveal the curious artistic blindness which sometimes made him the most Philistine of poets than in this lack of sensitiveness to the delicacy, the spiritual suggestiveness, the deep and essential privacy of relations which belong to the most intimate life and which become brutal the moment they become public.

The lack of fineness in Whitman, the insensibility to the appeal of the spiritual qualities of character, the absence of the note of distinction, are very obvious when one studies his work in its relation to women; there is nowhere any touch of the spiritual chivalry which nearly all the great poets have shared; no suggestion of the power of beautiful portraiture with which Homer, Dante, Shakespeare, and Goethe, for instance, have enriched the world with the images of Andromache, Beatrice, Rosalind, Gretchen. The " dream of fair women " seems never to have come to Whitman; if it had, he could

not possibly have treated the most intimate relation between men and women as if it were a
public function. There was a whole world of
poetry from which, by the limitation of his nature, this powerful man was excluded. And
this is the more singular because his was not a
purely masculine genius; there was a large infu-
sion of the feminine in it. It is not so much
sheer force and energy that impress one in
Whitman as a certain diffused softness of
feeling, a brooding affection, a seeking after
and celebration of brotherliness, comradeship;
most notably, in his striking and original treatment of death the element of tenderness is delicately and beautifully expressed.

So many and so various are the qualities which
Whitman reveals, so diverse are the moods with
which one reads him, that the very difficulty of
reaching a final judgment regarding his genius
and rank becomes an evidence of something unusual and commanding in the man. It is high
time, surely, to see him as he is; to escape the
blindness of those who have never been able to
find anything but the " barbaric yawp " in him,
and the idolatry of those who think that he has

A Byway in Huntington

abolished the laws of art. He was great in
mass and magnitude rather than in altitude and
quality; he had the richest endowment of imagination that has yet been bestowed on any
American poet, but his power of organizing it
into noble and beautiful forms was far below the
wealth of his material; he had an ear for the
fundamental rhythms, but he often disregarded
or violated his musical sense. He entered into
the broad, elemental life of the country and
caught its sweep of interest and occupation with
fresh and original power, disclosing at times a
passion of imagination which closely approaches
great poetry and predicts the great poetry which
will some day be written on this continent.
Here Whitman is at his best and stands out as,
in a very real sense, the distinctively American
poet—the devout lover of democracy and its
most ardent and eloquent singer. But even here
there are limitations to be observed; for Whitman speaks for a plane of society, not for its
entirety; he cares for and understands the elemental and basal types; he does not comprehend
nor recognize the sharing of the great human
qualities on a basis of equality by the more

highly developed types. And democracy, it must be remembered, does not mean the average man only; it means *all* men.

Whitman has a fundamentally religious view of life which makes him brother with all men and in sympathy with all experience; but he has no affinity with the higher and holier attainments of character; he fails to recognize the immense chasm which yawns between the saint and the deliberate and persistent sinner, which may be bridged hereafter, but which is, now and here, a tremendous fact. He is, at his best, master of a fresh, suggestive, deeply impressive phrase, which brings with it something of the immediate and convincing cogency and charm of nature; at his worst he is ponderous, prosaic, and eminently uninspired. When his inspiration ebbs, he stereotypes himself. He has written a little group of poems which are more distinctive and original than any others that have come from an American hand; he has written a vast mass of irregular verse which has no possible relation to poetry, and which ought, as a matter of justice to his genius and memory, to be separated from his real work and put into

Whitman's Grave at Camden

that storage-room to which most of the great writers have made unwilling contributions. After this has been done there will remain a small body of verse that is likely to last as long as anything in American poetry.

Abbotsford

THE LAND OF SCOTT

THE LAND OF SCOTT

R. LANG has said that, often as it has been his fortune to write about Sir Walter Scott, he has never sat down to do so without a sense of happiness and elation. " It is," he writes, " as if one were meeting a dear friend, or at least were to talk with other friends about him. This emotion is so strong, no doubt, because the name and memory and magic of Sir Walter are entwined with one's earliest recollections of poetry, and nature, and the vines and hills of home." It is easy, and of late years it has been a kind of literary convention, to emphasize the defects in Scott's work; its loose and often awk-

ward construction, the verbosity of the style, the lack of selection and the consequent overcrowding of the story, the carelessness of a born raconteur who has more incidents at command than he can wisely use. These faults are so obvious that it is unnecessary to recall them. There is, however, something humorous in the patronizing attitude of a little group of very modern, deft, expert framers of sentences toward this large, friendly, affluent mind, this warm, generous, gracious spirit, who shares with Shakespeare, Lope de Vega, Dumas, and Victor Hugo the indifference of the possessor of a great fortune to the details of his bequests to his kind. Scott ought to have been more studious of form, more fastidious of style; he ought to have written with more deliberation and revised with more rigor; but when all these defects are charged up against him, how heavily the language and the race remain indebted to him, and how painfully lacking in perception is the criticism which reports the shadows but ignores the light which streams from this greathearted man!

If the claim of the author of " Quentin Dur-

The Brig o' Turk

ward " to a large place in the literature of the English-speaking peoples could not be established by putting his works in evidence, the charm of his personality and the story of his heroic struggle to die with honor would invest him with a human and romantic interest of the kind which gives wings to certain names and sends them on a level flight with time.

The sensitiveness to form as form, the delicacy of taste in detail, the nice feeling for the subtle relations between thought and speech, the light touch on the magical elements in language, which constitute the artistic equipment of Poe, De Maupassant, Pater, and Henry James, are not to be found in Scott; he belongs to another order of artists, another class of those who minister to the needs of the spirit. Even these accomplished writers present large arid surfaces and are at times unconscionable offenders against the very taste they cultivate. Poe permits himself the most repulsive detail in the introduction of horrors from which the sensitive instinctively turn away; Mr. James was once described by a friendly critic of notable sanity as " on the whole, in places, the worst

writer of the time "; De Maupassant's moral
sense was so dulled that in his most delicate art
he sometimes gives his reader's normal instinct
a blow between the eyes without the slightest
consciousness that he has betrayed his defect
of insight; while Mr. Pater's essay on " Style "
is a terrible example of the way in which he
ought not to have done it. These subtle workers
in gold, ivory, and clay have their own place
and are getting more perhaps than their share
of honor from this generation; but those who
accept them as the final arbiters of form, the
ultimate court of appeal in all questions of style,
must make place for the less delicate but more
vital makers of imperishable images; for the
large, virile, fecund natures who, from Homer
to Tolstoi, have wrought with a certain careless
ease born of the consciousness of the command
of inexhaustible resources. If those lovers of
Scott whose taste is catholic but whose courage
is weak need the confirmation of the judgment
of the great, let them take heart in the companionship of Goethe, the first of literary critics, and
of Thackeray, one of the first of literary artists.

The root of Scott's offending is the root of

his greatness: he is not literary in the technical sense of the word. There is nothing professional about him; he is primarily a Scotch gentleman and landed proprietor. He has a natural, out-of-doors way with him which vitally relates him to his people and his country and makes him companionable to all sorts of people. It is not necessary to take a special course in the history of thought to understand him. He has no reform on his heart, save the ancient and honorable passion to make the rules of honor bear on all men's consciences and to set the ideals of courage and courtesy before every man's eyes. He was not bent on solving the problems of his time. He was fortunate enough to live in a time which did not confuse fiction with psychology. He did not write semi-historical romances because it was easy and profitable, but because his heart and imagination were equally under the spell of the rich store of Scottish legends and annals. He was, fortunately for us, a Tory, and the French Revolution confirmed his early bent. He was, in a word, in the best possible attitude to receive those elements out of early and contemporary life which gave his genius wings, and equipped him to set the spectacle of life before the world as he saw it through a vivacious, pictorial imagination.

Scott was not a subtle strategist in art, playing a deep game with his readers, employing a highly elaborate technique to produce delicate effects on a few elect minds; he always moves in the open, masses his forces, and wins his way by mass and force. He deals with those fundamental experiences which, being common to all men, are, by reason of their universality, the most inclusive and profound happenings that befall human kind; and his manner has the breadth and simplicity which are harmonious with his themes. The great movements which give color and direction to human affairs are neither set in motion nor controlled by finesse, dexterity, subtle suggestion; they have their source in wide stirrings of the conscience or of the imagination, and find leadership in capacious, virile minds. Scott was entirely lacking in subtlety, but subtlety is not depth; he was without finesse, but finesse is not power. Depth he had and power in abundance; he was deep not as the pools but as the ocean, and his power was not that of

St. Margaret's Loch and Arthur's Seat, Edinburgh

delicate mechanism, but of the large, elemental forces of nature.

A man of such broad, sincere, sane genius as Scott is always vitally related to his people and his country; for genius is a spiritual rather than an intellectual gift, and makes its richest contribution to thought through divination rather than by logical processes. As Homer divined what lay in the heart of his race, as Dante felt even more deeply than he understood the Spirit of the Middle Age, as Shakespeare read the secret records which life had written in the spirit of the race, so Scott, with less insight and dramatic power, but with kindred breadth of sympathy, comprehended his country and people and made himself their foremost interpreter and historian. For Scotland lives in the books of her great romancer as she lives in no work of history. What has happened *to* her may be read elsewhere; what has happened *in* her must be sought in the Waverley Novels and the poems from the same hand.

Scott found practically all his material ready to his hand, and so intimately is his work associated with Scottish scenery, history, and legend that the bare record of the points of contact would exceed the limits of this comment on the background against which Rob Roy, Di Vernon, Jeanie Deans, Claverhouse, Meg Merrilies, Bonnie Prince Charlie, and a host of figures with whom the English-speaking peoples have long lived on terms of intimacy, move and have their being. To place the men and women whom Scott created or recalled in their local environment one must have at hand a history and a map of Scotland; it must suffice here to emphasize the importance of the background as an element in Scott's work.

It is in childhood that the intimacies of the imagination are most easily established, and nothing enters into the background of an artist's work until it has been assimilated by the imagination. Familiarity with places, with outlooks, with the richest associations, does not of itself create the mood in which a man enlarges the horizons of his consciousness so to include his surroundings that they become part of his unconscious as well as of his conscious life; to the sense of sight must be added vision; to the intimacy of physical acquaintance must be added the knowledge that comes with brooding over enchanting or impressive scenes, the meditation that opens the heart of a legend. As a boy and youth Scott became first familiar and then intimate with the country and the history of Scotland.

A great career is always the consummation of a long course of preparation, and the base of Scott's achievement was laid by his ancestry. He came of the right stock; the blood of romancers ran in his veins. If he had inherited a family memory, it would have rung with the shouts of ancient border warfare, with the cries of the clans, with all the tumult of Highland life. He was kinsman of the Campbells, the Macdonalds, the Rutherfords, the Hardens, the great feudal house of Buccleuch. He spoke humorously of the Scotchman's respect for his pedigree in the fragment of autobiography, but when he built Abbotsford he had the armorial bearings of his ancestors emblazoned on the ceiling of the great hall. The social importance of his descent was a minor matter compared with its possible bequest to his imagination.

He was not only born in the ranks of the

men of romance, but in one of the most romantic cities of the Old World. Always gray and often somber in the fogs and dim wintry twilights of the far north, Edinburgh takes rank with Florence and Venice among the cities which appeal not only to the imagination by reason of a history rich in audacity, in picturesque incident, and in mysterious tragedy, but to the eye by reason of beauty of situation, nobility of structure, distinction of individuality. The great commercial cities, as a rule, run out in long lines or spread themselves over vast level areas; Edinburgh seems always visible to the eye in its entirety, so nobly do the hills rise about it crowned with castle and monument. One can stand in the heart of the Scottish capital and see it not only spread out but rising about him in impressive lines.

The city of to-day is vastly changed from the old town in which the novelist was born on August 15, 1771; there are beautiful gardens and broad streets where he may have played over open fields; but the Castle still frowns on the hill as in the earlier times, and the street runs precipitously down to St. Giles through lofty

Edinburgh Castle

buildings in which the old wynds are still found; and Holyrood sits amid the ruins, and Calton Hill, with the High School on its slope and crowned by the unfinished line of Doric columns, not only adds a strikingly picturesque feature to the city, but interprets and symbolizes its high quality of intellectual life, its ancient and loyal devotion to learning.

The Edinburgh of to-day includes a new city, built up since Scott was born, along the base of the old city. In Princes Street this New Town has the most picturesque thoroughfare through which the tides of life ebb and flow. Its breadth, the solidity and harmony of the buildings that line it on one side, and the beautiful gardens that give it the freshness and charm of foliage and sward on the other; the great cliff rising abruptly beyond, with the Castle on the summit, the impressive monuments and public buildings, impart to modern Edinburgh a dignity and distinction entirely its own.

The New Town and Scott were born about the same time, but the associations of his youth center in the picturesque Old Town. Here, as everywhere in this irreverent modern world intent on convenience and not scrupulous about landmarks, radical changes have been made since 1771; but High Street still runs its steep course from the Castle to St. Giles, and there, of a Sunday morning, the swirl of the pipes is still heard as the Highlanders come swinging down, with flying tartans, to the military service. " A sloping high street and many side lanes, covering like some wrought tissue of stone and mortar, like some rhinoceros skin, with many a gnarled embossment, church steeple, chimney head, Tolbooth and other ornament or indispensability, back and ribs of the slope " —to recall Carlyle's description of the place as he saw it in his youth.

Many destructive changes had already been made, but then as now the conformation and character of the town are clearly discernible. The narrow thoroughfares, the lofty stone buildings, the dark closes, the crowding of the population on the ridge of the great rock, made old Edinburgh an extension of its Castle. A rock of refuge and a place of defense, with the Castle at one end and the Abbey at the other, it was proudly defiant of the Highlands to the north

whence bands of ravagers descended and swept
the land as the Norsemen the shores of France
in the days before Rollo, and of the Border on
the south, full of unrest and turbulence.

If the enchantments of the Middle Age did not
invest the Edinburgh into which Scott was born,
the wild, romantic history of centuries of struggle had left their records on every side. It was
a veritable citadel of ancient tradition; nowhere
else in Europe are population and historical
association more congested. The old fifteen-
story buildings, the forerunners of the great
business structures of to-day, have disappeared,
but ten stories still tower above the narrow closes
and wynds, and armorial bearings, antique door-
handles, link-extinguishers, carven finials, half-
erased dates and inscriptions, are still to be
found. Foul with the surviving odors of the
evil-smelling Middle Age, full of squalor re-
deemed by touches of splendor, dark and
gloomy but rich in haunting memories, the
city which held in its heart St. Giles and the
Old Tolbooth—the "Heart of Midlothian"—
was a veritable fairyland to a boy of Scott's pictorial imagination. Born of an ancestry which

included the " Bould Rutherfords that were sae
stout," William Boltfoot of Harden, always the
first " to tak the foord," the " Flower of Yarrow," whose sweetness lives in song, it was
Scott's great good fortune to open his eyes on a
world which preserved the records of the age
of which he was to be the chief recorder, to
store his memory and stimulate his imagination
in those sensitive years in which a man instinctively reaches after the things which belong to
his temperament and genius, and takes them to
himself without knowing that he is making
ready for his work.

The son of a " Writer to the Signet," with
a fondness for " analyzing the abstruse feudal
doctrines connected with conveyancing," Scott
was born not far from the heart of the Old
Town, in a house which stood at the head
of College Wynd, then a fashionable quarter.
Here Oliver Goldsmith had once lived in the
days of his study at the University, and through
this street in Scott's infancy Boswell conducted
Dr. Johnson to the University. The house in
which the senior Walter Scott lived was pulled
down to make room for the present University

Loch Achray and Ben Venue

building, which was begun in 1789 and completed nearly half a century later.

The death of six children in rapid succession gave ground for the suspicion that College Wynd was not a wholesome locality, and shortly after the birth of the future novelist the family removed to George's Square, a more open section of the town, of which Lord Cockburn writes: "With its pleasant, trim-kept gardens, it has an air of antiquated grandeur about it, and retains not a few traces of its former dignity and seclusion." Here, in a neighborhood crowded with historical and literary associations and memories, Walter Scott lived during his boyhood and youth and well on into his early manhood. He could not walk the few squares to his first school in Bristo Street, or, later, to the high, narrow building in the High School Yards, or, still later, to the "Town's College," as the University was called, without being assailed from every quarter by the memories of great men or of those great events which wait upon great men.

Before he was two years old, Scott lost the use of his right leg, as the result of an illness, in a way that baffled the skill of the physicians, and was sent to his grandfather's farm, Sandy-Knowe, in order to secure better and freer conditions. The village of Smailholm, in Roxburgh-shire, was then a small hamlet, in that Scottish Border, of which the poet and romancer took such complete possession by the power of his imagination that it has become "the Scott Country" for all time: the home of romance and poetry, through which the Tweed flows, dear to all the world because its murmur was music in the ears of the broken but heroic man who came home to Abbotsford to die in 1832.

Smailholm lies on a ridge and commands a wide landscape to the Cheviot Hills and the slopes of Lammermoor. In the simple farmhouse the "puir lame laddie" was tenderly watched over, and there he heard for the first time, with conscious interest, those stories of daring and of achievement which were to form the richest material of his education. In a volume of Ramsay's "Tea Table Miscellany" in the library at Abbotsford he wrote: "This book belonged to my grandfather, Robert Scott, and out of it I was taught 'Hardy Knute' by heart long before I could read the ballad myself. It was the first poem I ever learned—the last I shall ever forget."

The countryside was rich in romantic association, and the list of its localities to-day reads like a résumé of Scott's life and work. Mertown's Halls; the Brethren Stanes; Dryburgh, where Scott and Lockhart sleep together in one of those burial-places the very loveliness of which is a symbol of immortality; the landmarks of Yarrow and Ettrick; the peaks of Peeblesshire; the crags of Hume; the vale of the Gala; "such were the objects," writes Lockhart, "that had painted the earliest images on the eye of the last and greatest of the Border Minstrels."

It was in the farm-house at Smailholm that Scott first became conscious that he was in the world and a very considerable part of it, and one of his earliest recollections was lying on the floor of the little parlor, "stripped and swathed up in a sheepskin, warm as it was flayed from the carcass of the animal." The child's grandmother was a repository of Scottish legend and tradition, in whose youth the stories of the Border depredations were matters of comparatively recent history. She told him many a tale of Watt of Harden, Jamie Telfer of the Fair Dodhead, and heroes of kindred spirit—"merry men all, of the persuasion and calling of Robin Hood and Little John." A very pretty picture of Scott at this earliest period remains in the record of an acquaintance of the grandparents: "Old Mrs. Scott sitting, with her spinning-wheel, at one side of the fire, in a *clean, clean* parlor; the grandfather, a good deal failed, in his elbow-chair opposite; and the little boy lying on the carpet at the old man's feet, listening to the Bible, or whatever good book Miss Jennie was reading to them." Miss Jennie was one of those invaluable aunts whose happy fortune it is to read fairy stories to children and to be always touched with the glow of romance which streams from their fascinating pages.

In his fourth year the boy was taken to Bath in pursuit of strength. He had gained greatly in general vigor, and his life was probably saved by the prompt and thorough measures taken by his father. He had lived largely in the open air, and those fine days when he was carried out

Dryburgh Abbey

and laid on the rocks by the old shepherd while the sheep browsed around them had invigorated his body while they nourished his imagination. He now became a sturdy child, with a slight limp, but able to share to the full the pleasures of exercise and of sport. In London he saw the Tower and Westminster Abbey, but the chief incident of this first journey and residence in England was a night at the theater, where he saw "As You Like It." Years afterward he wrote that the witchery of the whole scene was still alive in his mind; and he remembered being so much scandalized at the quarrel between Orlando and his brother in the first scene that he cried out, " A'n't they brothers? " Later he recalled with pleasure the Parade in Bath, with the winding Avon, the lowing of cattle on the opposite hills, and the splendors of a certain shop in the town. He was afflicted at this time by a superstitious fear of statuary, and was cured of this failing by familiarity with a statue of Neptune which stood beside the river.

There were rapid changes of place in the search for health during the next few months, and the boy's time was unevenly divided between

Edinburgh, Sandy-Knowe, and Prestonpans. It was at this time that an accomplished lady, after spending a night in the home in George's Square, wrote these prophetic words to a friend the following day: " I last night supped in Mr. Walter Scott's. He has the most extraordinary genius of a boy I ever saw. He was reading a poem to his mother when I went in. I made him read on; it was the description of a shipwreck. His passion rose with the storm. He lifted his eyes and hands. ' There's the mast gone,' says he; ' crash it goes!—they all perish! ' After his agitation he turns to me. ' That is too melancholy,' says he; ' I had better read you something more amusing.' I preferred a little chat, and asked his opinion of Milton and other books he was reading, which he gave me wonderfully." At Prestonpans he had the good fortune to make the acquaintance of a veteran who was resting in the village on half-pay after his campaigns, and who found in the boy an eager and patient listener, with an insatiable appetite for tales of adventure and descriptions of military feats.

After a short attendance at a private school

in Edinburgh, and, later, instruction at the hands of a tutor, Scott's formal education was begun in the High School, where he describes himself as popular by reason of his good nature and ready imagination, but much given to frivolity and neglect of study. He had already begun to write verses, chiefly remarkable, as youthful verses often are, for piety and lack of inspiration:

ON A THUNDER-STORM

Loud o'er my head though awful thunders roll,
And vivid lightnings flash from pole to pole,
Yet 't is thy voice, my God, that bids them fly,
Thy arm directs those lightnings through the sky;
Then let the good thy mighty name revere,
And hardened sinners thy just vengeance fear.

This didactic mood, so normal in an undeveloped boy, was humanized by wholesome activity; for Scott was " more distinguished in the yards than in the class." The boy had early resolved not to let his lameness stand in the way of a free and vigorous physical life, and before he left the High School he had become one of the boldest and surest-footed climbers of " the kittle nine stanes," a perilous passage on the face of the Castle rock.

The interval between leaving the High School and entering the University was spent with the aunt who had already had so large a place in his vital education, in a cottage at Kelso. He was then twelve years old, and at the age when the imagination is most easily stirred and impressed. His surroundings during those impressionable months left ineffaceable images in his memory, and had no small place in his preparation for his work. He described Kelso as the " most beautiful if not the most romantic village in Scotland, presenting objects not only grand in themselves, but venerable for their associations." The cottage stood in a garden, with long paths between hedges of yew and hornbeam; there were thickets of flowering shrubs, a bower, and an arbor accessible only through a labyrinth. Chief among the trees of the garden was a great platanus under which the boy took a long leap in his education when " Percy's Reliques " fell into his hands for the first time. He attended the Grammar School at Kelso during this period, but his real teacher was the

The Canongate Tolbooth, Edinburgh

noble country about him, through which he walked with the energy of an explorer and the joy of a poet. Two rivers, beautiful in themselves and flowing out of the fairyland of Scottish song and story,—the Tweed and the Teviot, —were close at hand; ancient and picturesque ruins were within reach. He was fast coming to his own, though he did not know it until years later, and he was instinctively taking to himself the stuff of life in nature and books which was to enrich his spirit and give his genius strength of wing.

He found the most fascinating and, in a way, the most liberating of all his text-books in the Kelso library, and read them out-of-doors in the shade of a plane-tree. " I remember well the spot," he wrote later, " where I read those volumes for the first time. It was beneath a huge platanus, in the ruins of what had been intended for an old-fashioned arbor in the garden I have mentioned. The summer day sped onward so fast that, notwithstanding the sharp appetite of thirteen, I forgot the hour of dinner, was sought for with anxiety, and was still found entranced in my intellectual banquet. To read, to remember, was in this instance the same thing, and henceforth I overwhelmed my school-fellows, and all who would hearken to me, with tragical recitations from the ballads of Bishop Percy. The first time, too, I could scrape a few shillings together, which were not common occurrences with me, I bought unto myself a copy of these beloved volumes; nor do I believe I ever read a book half so frequently or with half the enthusiasm." This was perhaps the most significant moment in Scott's education, as was the reading of Spenser's " Faerie Queene " in the education of Keats.

James Ballantyne, whose acquaintance, made at this time, was probably the most momentous happening in his external life, tells us that during this period Scott was devoted to antiquarian lore and was the best story-teller he ever knew. " He soon discovered that I was as fond of listening as he himself was of relating; and I remember it was a thing of daily occurrence that, after he had made himself master of his own lesson, I, alas, being still sadly to seek in mine, he used to whisper to me, ' Come, slink over beside me, Jamie, and I 'll tell you a story.' " And

THE LAND OF SCOTT

Scott has been inviting the world for eighty years to sit beside him and listen, and the magic is still potent.

He has left a very definite report of the deep joy which entered his soul in those days of his dawning intellectual life, the glow of his imagination, under the spell of the beauty of the Border and of its romantic associations. From this time the love of natural beauty, especially when associated with ancient splendor, became a passion with him.

In November, 1783, Scott entered the Humanity and Greek classes in the University of Edinburgh; but these formal studies did not interrupt the education which, by the instinct of genius, he had marked out for himself. Every Saturday, and more frequently during vacations, he was in the habit of climbing Salisbury Crags, Arthur's Seat, or Blackford Hill, with a bundle of books from the circulating library; and in the silence and solitude of the summit, Edinburgh at their feet, the Firth in the distance, the bluebells about them, and the shadows resting on the Pentland hills, these boys read together Spenser, Ariosto, Boiardo, and the other

masters of the romantic mood. This habit, kept
up for several years, made Scott so familiar with
stories of knight-errantry and of romantic love
and adventure that he could recite them from
memory by the hour. In this extra-university
fashion, after the manner of boys of talent since
colleges began, Scott learned Italian until he
could read it with ease, and began a collection of
ballads of which six volumes are preserved in
the library at Abbotsford. He learned enough
Spanish to read and enjoy "Don Quixote."
Pulci, the Decameron, Brantôme, he knew; and
Froissart, it is hardly necessary to say, he had
at his fingers' ends. He fastened like a tiger,
he tells us, on any collection of old songs and
romances that came in his way. Of his intellectual interests and occupations at this period
he probably gives a faithful account in " Waverley ": " In English literature, he was master of Shakespeare and Milton, of our earlier
dramatic authors, of many picturesque and
interesting passages from our old historical
chronicles, and was particularly well acquainted
with Spenser, Drayton, and other poets, who
have exercised themselves on romantic fiction,—
of all themes the most fascinating to a youthful

Loch Katrine

imagination, before the passions have roused themselves and demand poetry of a more sentimental description." James Sibbald's circulating library in the Parliament Square had more to do with Scott's education, it may be suspected, than the University; and what the library could not teach he learned on the Tweedside and in the Highlands.

The details of Scott's career at the Bar, as a translator, editor, poet, and, finally, as a novelist, would be out of place in this endeavor to bring into clear relief the background of his work by showing the great part which it played in his education. Notwithstanding his lameness, he was one of the most active men of his time in most forms of exercise. During his High School and University days he came to know the country about Edinburgh by heart, in numberless long walks. Later he wandered farther afield on foot or on horseback, and his father began to protest that he was becoming a strolling peddler. His principal object in these long excursions, he tells us, was the pleasure of seeing romantic scenery and of visiting localities associated with historical events.

Wandering over the battle-field of Bannock-

burn gave him deeper delight than the noble
view from the walls of Stirling Castle, not because the sweep of that great landscape did not
appeal to him, but because his interest in all historical memorials was so keen and his genius for
discovering their significance so great. " Show
me an old castle or a battle-field and I was at
home at once, filled it with its combatants in their
proper costume, and overwhelmed my hearers
by the enthusiasm of my description." Such
glimpses into Scott's mind bring into clear light
the sincerity and integrity of his selection of
his material. The age and genius of chivalry,
the habit and costume of feudalism, were as real
and vital to him as were the standards and manners of the society in which Becky Sharp lived
to Thackeray, or as the " form and pressure "
of the life of the hour is to the most uncom-
promising of contemporary realists.

Scott's acquaintance with the Border was
intimate and began with his earliest childhood;
his knowledge of the Highlands probably dates
from his fifteenth year. His first excursion into
a region which was still distant and wild was
made in the autumn of 1786 or 1787, as the guest

of an ardent Jacobite of Invernahyde, who had taken part in the risings of 1715 and 1745, whose loyalty to the exiled house of Scotland was a steady flame, and who, in his old age, cherished the hope of drawing his claymore once more before he died. Never was a writer of romantic temper more fortunate than was Scott on this memorable visit to the section whose tragic story he was to write with inimitable pathos and humor. It was a true journey of discovery; a veritable conquest of the imagination. When the vale of Perth first opened before him, he tells us that he pulled up the reins without meaning to do so and gazed on the scene as if he were afraid it would shift, like the scenes in a theater, before he could distinctly observe its different parts, or convince himself that what he saw was real.

But still deeper was the delight with which he listened to the stories of his enthusiastic host, who was not only the custodian of the history and legends of the Highlands, but the incarnation of the intrepid and romantic temper of the Highlander. From the lips of this veteran of the last heroic stand for a lost cause and a fallen house in Scotland the future author of " Wa-

verley " and " Rob Roy " listened spellbound
to the moving tale of the campaigns with Mar
and Charles Edward; of his hiding in a rocky
cave not far from his own house, which was in
the hands of English troops, after the battle of
Culloden; of his broadsword duel with Rob Roy;
of a hundred other incidents which fired the
boy's heart and stored his memory with romantic material.

Year after year these expeditions into the
wilder parts of Scotland were repeated, until
Scott came to have not only complete knowledge
of the topography of the Highlands and of the
coast, but to carry in his mind a kind of historical and legendary map of Scotland in which all
the centers of story and points of interest in
the Border and the Highlands were distinctly
marked.

His first sight of Loch Katrine, which he was
to endear to the whole world, was gained under
military escort, while he was a writer's appren-
tice and on legal business, the little cavalcade
being in charge of a sergeant who was a repository of local traditions. These raids, as Scott
called them, gave him acquaintance not only

Melrose Abbey

THE LAND OF SCOTT

with the country but with people of every rank
and condition, and with the rich fund of song
and story that floated about Scotland from
vale to vale and from farthest Sutherlandshire
to the English border. To know men who had
known Rob Roy, to hear the story of the two
risings which had shaken Scotland like an earth-
quake, to be a guest in remote and lonely castles,
to be guided through wild defiles and over vast
mountain ranges by kilted clansmen whose only
speech was Gaelic and whose claymores were
still at the service of their chiefs—this was the
real education of the writer who was to be the
scribe of his country, the truest of her historians.
He had taken the hand of the man who sent
the fiery cross through Appin before the last
and most tragic pouring out of fanatical loyalty
in the Highlands; he had a portrait of Prince
Charles, purchased by some of his earliest sav-
ings; there was still a " king over the sea," and
many were the glasses that were dashed to the
floor after his health had been drunk in Scottish
castles and homes; the heroic age was still so
near that its glow had not faded from the imagination: surely no poet and romancer was

more fortunately born than the author of " The Lady of the Lake " and of the romances which bear on their title-pages the name of Walter Scott!

The Highlands had a large place in Scott's imagination, as they have in his novels, but his heart was in the Border, and Ruskin was well within the truth when he wrote: " Scott's life was, in all the joyful strength of it, spent in the valley of the Tweed. Rosebank, in the Lower Tweed, gave him his close knowledge of the district of Flodden Field, and his store of foot-traveler's interest in every glen of Ettrick, Yarrow, and Liddel Water." Smailholm and Kelso were among his earliest homes, and when he chose the place which of all others appealed to him most he turned instinctively to the banks of the Tweed.

Scott saw Abbotsford in his mind's eye long before the first stone had been laid. Not far from the place where the house stands the last of the great battles between the clans was fought in 1526, and the elder Walter Scott went over the ground with the future Laird when the latter was still a boy. In 1811 the boy, become a man of distinction and considerable fortune, purchased the farm property of Cartleyhole, with a small house fast going to decay. No place could have offered more, however, to the man who saw the locality not only with his eyes but with his imagination. The Tweed flowed through the very heart of the landscape, gentle hills gathered about it, the glens of Ettrick and Yarrow were within reach, and Melrose and Dryburgh were not distant.

To-day the whole region seems like a page in the life of the builder of Abbotsford; but during the first years of his ownership the most unambitious designs were in his mind. In 1812 he wrote to Byron: "I am laboring here to contradict an old proverb, and make a silk purse out of a sow's ear, namely, to convert a bare hough and brae into a comfortable farm." In thirteen years the cottage became a castle and the farm an estate; and this transformation had involved the expenditure of great sums of money. At Christmas in 1824 the completion of the castle was celebrated by a great house-warming.

For a time Scott was supremely happy; he

had a noble estate in the heart of the country he loved; his house was a museum of antiquarian objects; he had a fine library; guests came and went in long procession. Into the house, as into everything to which he set his hand, Scott put his heart; it was the expression of all the manifold interests of his life: "Abbotsford was reared on no set plan, but with the desire to reproduce some of those features of ancient Scottish architecture which Scott most venerated. It was at once a monument of the high historical imagination from which sprang his more enduring memorial, and of the over-zeal which may be lavished, with very disastrous results, on the mere 'pomp and circumstance of time' —the all-absorbing passion

> "To call this wooded patch of earth his own,
>   And rear the pile of ill-assorted stone,
>   And play the grand old feudal lord again."

In the dining-room he hung the portraits of his ancestors, and there, on a quiet autumn afternoon in 1832, the brave struggle over, the end came: "A beautiful day, so warm that my window was wide open, and so perfectly still that

The Quadrangle, Edinburgh University

the sound of all others most delicious to his ear—
the gentle ripple of the Tweed over its pebbles—
was distinctly audible as we knelt around the
bed, and his eldest son kissed and closed his
eyes." From that sacred place and scene came
a word which the world will never forget—the
last word to Lockhart: " Be a good man, my
dear."

It has been charged against Scott, in the years
of reaction against the romantic spirit in fiction,
that he is the painter of the life and manners of
Feudalism, and therefore a dealer in fictitious
values, a vender of obsolete wares. But nothing
that was once real and vital is ever less than real
and vital to the genius that penetrates to its
heart and revitalizes it. In this sense " Quentin Durward " is as genuine and sincere as
" Vanity Fair " or " Eugénie Grandet." Shakespeare is a better historian of Cleopatra, if the
chief function of history is to make the dead
live again, than Plutarch; and Scott is not to
be counted less authoritative because he was a recorder of life after the fact instead of contemporaneous with it. Nor must it be forgotten
that it was the soul of Feudalism which appealed

to his imagination; "the spirit of chivalry, by which, as by a vivifying soul, that system was animated," "founded on generosity and self-denial."

But Scott's absorption in feudalism has been greatly exaggerated; he was the delineator of chivalry in only three or four stories; in the great body of his work he was the recorder and interpreter of Scotland. In those romances Scotland lives in scores of men and women who are blood of her blood and bone of her bone. To recall these romances is to summon those fair apparitions in whom the pathos and tragedy of Scottish life are preserved against the touch of time: Jeanie and Effie Deans, Bessie Maclure, Di Vernon, Marie Stuart, Flora MacIvor, Lucy Ashton. In those pages live and move a long line of kings, gypsies, lawyers, preachers, judges, soldiers, farmers; men of the Border and of the Highlands, who not only keep for us the features of a past age, but reveal to us the secret of the heroism, the prodigal loyalty, the dour ruggedness, and the deep tenderness which have made Scotland the home of poetry and romance.

HAWTHORNE IN THE NEW
WORLD

HAWTHORNE IN THE NEW
WORLD

UR literature is singular in
that, alone among the lit-
eratures of the greater races,
it had beginnings but no
youth; it was born highly
sophisticated, if not full-
grown. Its strength lies in
vigor of conviction rather than in depth of experience; in definiteness of aim rather than in
rich spontaneity; in moderation, poise, and integrity rather than in passion, tidal flood of
energy, surrender to imperious moods. It is,
so far, the record of a clear-minded, idealistic
people, bent on executive rectitude, rather than
of a people deeply moved by the mystery and

pathos of life, stirred by impulses which rise from the instincts and are stronger than reason, swept out of its moorings from time to time by mysterious currents from unexplored tracts of its nature. This does not mean that Americans are commonplace; it does mean that their art has not, save in rare moments, caught and held the force and splendor of elemental passion.

The Jews began the written record of their experience, both in idea and in action, with reports of cosmic forces subdued to high ends, and of men stirring into life with immense vitality; the Greeks told the story of a great war set in motion by a passion for a beautiful woman; the Germans recited moving tales of gods and men, with swords bared in a thousand hours of reckless measuring of strength with strength; the English brought with them the legend of a hero slaying a monster; the French beguiled the slow-moving hours of the Middle Ages with the doings of Alexander, of Charlemagne, of Arthur; the Spaniards fed their youth with the brave adventures of the Cid; while the Irish were loving without counting the cost, and fighting for the sport of it, as far back as the time of

Cuchulain. In epic, ballad, lyric, and story, the first records of the older races have to do with reckless fighting, audacious adventure, lawless and uncalculating passion.

Our writing begins, on the other hand, with the reports of men who had put romance away with resolute hands, and were determined to achieve definite and rational ends in a New World; who were not without awe of its mystery, but who were chiefly concerned to get it under tillage, and to turn its resources to practical account. Our literature of fiction begins with " Ethan Brand," " Peter Rugg," " The Fall of the House of Usher," " Wieland; or, the Transformation " ! The significance of these facts has not yet been fully disclosed; when it is we shall understand Poe and Hawthorne better.

The ancestors of Hawthorne left England while the memory of Shakespeare and his contemporaries was still fresh; the settlers of the next century might have read Fielding and Smollett in the first editions; but in Hawthorne, Emerson, Poe, and Irving there is no hint of the sixteenth-century passion or of the unashamed virility of the eighteenth century. A sudden maturity seems to have descended on the men of the New World. Puritanism had sublimated life by denying some of its instincts and putting others outside the pale of written speech; and harassing dangers and inexorable work gave elemental impulses safe channels of expression. The men of New England were engrossed by the necessity of saving their souls, and the men of Virginia and South Carolina by the pleasure of a free, hospitable, active, out-of-door life. There were intellectual interests, scholarly traditions, and well-read libraries North and South; but life was essentially practical, and art kept company with none of the early emigrants from the Old to the New World.

The New World was so new that all the rudimentary work of civilization had to be done over again; it was without accumulations of legend, romance, learning, religion, or society; everything had to be made out of hand. This work was done by several hundred thousand families, forming a long and often defenseless skirmish-line in a country full of unorganized but relentless enemies. These families came from different countries, or from different classes of society. They had little acquaintance with one another, and in that period absence of knowledge meant presence of suspicion and distrust. The means of communication were few, the distances great, and travel was slow, laborious, and expensive. When Hawthorne, Emerson, and Poe were born, these scattered communities had taken on a formal unity as the result of a struggle for the right to manage their own affairs, and they had acted together for three or four decades rather by force of circumstances than by reason of any deep sense of community of feeling or of aims. The former colonists were living under one government, but they had not become a nation.

The prophetic sense in Emerson divined the national idea long before it had taken deep root or found clear expression in the minds of his contemporaries; but Hawthorne and Poe, being primarily, and by the compulsion of a positive if somewhat sublimated genius, artists, and concerned largely with the forms of things, had no such divination; and while both had behind them the distinctive and highly organized life of sections, neither had the ample background, nor

was either fed by the deep and rich influences,
of a highly developed national life. Hawthorne
was a New-Englander rather than an American;
there were few Americans in his time. " At
present," he writes, "we have no country, at
least none in the sense an Englishman has a
country. I never conceived, in reality, what a
true and warm love of country is till I witnessed
it in the breasts of Englishmen. The States are
too various and extended to form really one
country. New England is quite as large a lump
of earth as my heart can really take in." In
Poe there is no hint of the wealth of association,
memory, and experience, capitalized by a race
which has lived together for centuries, which one
feels in Chaucer or Tennyson; in Hawthorne
there is no suggestion of the deep, rich movement of an old society which one feels in Balzac,
in Thackeray and Tourgenieff. The absence of
national consciousness, and of those forces which
flow with tidal volume through great communities and make them as one in the crises of experience, and the absorption of men in practical
affairs, are factors of the first importance in any
endeavor to understand or estimate the work of

IN THE NEW WORLD

Hawthorne, Emerson, and Poe, the most important figures in American literature.

Neither Hawthorne nor Poe touched the life of his time; nor, for that matter, did they touch with the bare hand the life of any time. Poe made his own world, fashioning it out of fantasy as boldly as he shaped the men and women of his imagination. We seem always to be looking at Hawthorne's figures from a distance; we never touch hands with them; they never speak directly to us; we do not expect to come upon them in any of those chance meetings which sometimes bring us face to face with Becky Sharp, Maggie Tulliver, and Silas Lapham. Even in " The Blithedale Romance " or " The Marble Faun," where we are within speaking and hearing distance, the drama unfolds before us in a silence as deep as that which infolds " The Scarlet Letter." Emerson spoke to the soul of his countrymen with the sustained nobility of deep insight and the persuasive eloquence of a very noble and sane outlook on life in its integrity and wholeness; but in Emerson it is altitude rather than mass which gives his work its spiritual distinction. He was not unaware of

311

a certain thinness of tone in it, a certain lack of mass; for he notes in himself what he calls " lack of constitution."

There was no lack of sensitive genius in Emerson, Hawthorne, or Poe, but there were distinct deficiencies in their background and in their period; to none of them did a rich national life give its fullness of power, its broad, deep humanness; to none of them did a warm, infolding air of sympathy bring its liberating force, its benignant and fertilizing influence. Emerson wrote much about his age, but chiefly about its possibilities; he escaped habitually into the upper air from the pressure of its hard conditions. Poe gives no hint anywhere, save in a few critical discussions, that he had any concern with the movements of his time or any interest in them. Hawthorne was a close and shrewd observer; but when his imagination begins to play, he is off and away as instinctively as the poet of most vagrant genius.

For all these writers, and especially for Hawthorne and Poe, art was a refuge from a country which did not feed the imagination, and a life which did not lend itself readily to imaginative

interpretation. If there had been literary scholars in America at the beginning of the nineteenth century, they would probably have pre-
dicted a literature of heroic figures, of the
idealization of action, of realistic devotion to
fact and force; instead of this reproduction in
art of provincial and local activities and energies,
there came a literature notable chiefly for its
detachment from actualities, its sublimation of
passion, its purity and distinction. Not until
our own time has the American writer begun
to deal at first hand and with his whole heart
with contemporary conditions in this country.
"Uncle Tom's Cabin" and other stories which
seem at first glance to refute this statement
really confirm it; not one of these stories was
written with the eye on the facts of life, or for
the love of those facts.

Isolated by the fact that his genius was of
greater capacity than the volume of life about
him, and that it was of a delicacy and subtlety
which that life could not furnish with congenial
material, Hawthorne was isolated also by the
force of ancestral facts, and by his temperament. He has left an impression of his ances-

tors which is at once curiously impersonal and
intensely personal; from the first emigrant who
bore his name, "grave, bearded, sable-cloaked
and steeple-crowned," treading the streets with
a stately port, with his Bible and his sword· his
son, so conspicuous in the persecution of the
witches that "their blood may fairly be said to
have left a stain upon him"; to the hardy ship-
masters of a later century, who began active life
before the mast and retired to the leisure of comfortable age from the quarter-deck. There were
survivals of all these ancestors in Hawthorne;
landsman as he was, he was rarely out of hearing
of the sea; the only practical occupations to
which he put his hand kept him on or near the
wharfs, and the notes of his consular experience
betray his constant interest in sailors and his instinctive feeling of relationship with them. It
was, however, by the earlier and sterner men of
his name that his imagination was most deeply
attracted. Removed from them by generations
of seafaring experience, liberated from their
intense and provincial ideas of life and duty, he
lived in and through the experiences of his Puritan ancestors with the marvelous penetration

of a genius of rare psychologic affinities and insight. " I know not whether those ancestors of mine," he writes, " bethought themselves to repent, and ask pardon of heaven for their cruelties; or whether they are now groaning under the heavy consequences of them, in another state of being. At all events, I, the present writer, as their representative, hereby take shame upon myself for their sakes, and pray that any curse incurred by them—as I have heard, and as the dreary and unprosperous condition of the race, for many a long year back, would argue to exist —may be now and henceforth removed."

Isolation was a potent fact in those impressionable years when he was finding himself and coming slowly into possession of his imagination and of the materials with which he was to work. The twelve years in the little room under the eaves in his mother's house in Salem, from 1825 to 1837, included the entire period of his earliest maturity, from his twenty-first to his thirty-third year. While most youths of genius were getting acquainted with life through experience, he was looking at it from a distance and with meditative eyes. Of action as a form of self-expression he knew nothing at a time when action solicits and compels the great majority of men.

He was not only shut off from his fellows, spending long days in reading, or dreaming, or composing and taking his walks at night, but he was separated from his own family. The emphasis on personality, which was the note of the Puritan view of life and the source of its strength and weakness, has produced a peculiar type of morbid character in New England, the distinguishing mark of which is its passion for solitude. In the South, where the social instinct has been highly developed, the " crank " is found at the post-office and the country store; in New England he lives by himself on the outskirts of the village, or in some lonely farmhouse; and the New England communities are few in which no hermit is found.

During the long years of her widowhood, Hawthorne's mother not only lived apart from the world, but from the members of her own family. His sisters followed their mother's example and lived in their own rooms. In such a ghostly atmosphere the young man succumbed

to the prevailing habit, and his meals were often
left at his locked door and eaten without human
fellowship in the solitude of his room. "We do
not even *live* at our house," he once said. In
the morning he studied, in the afternoon he
wrote, and in the evening he read; neither visitors nor friends knocked at his door. Delight in
the sense of being at home and in the opportunities for reading and dreaming gave the early
years of this monastic life keen interest, and contributed not a little to the fostering of his rare
genius and his delicate and sensitive talent; but,
as time passed, the monotony of his life, its un-
natural isolation, involving the denial of the instincts of his youth, bore heavily on his spirits,
and bred a depression that chilled his imagination and checked the creative impulse in him.
Driven back upon himself by the lack of a warm,
compelling life about him, such as bore Shakespeare on a flood-tide to the largest prosperity
of growth and art; finding nothing in the plain,
sincere, but unimaginative community in which
he lived to absorb or vitalize his imagination;
denied his share in the sympathy and genial
warmth of normal family life, Hawthorne took

317

refuge in a world which was full of moral reality, but which was as remote from the actual world as if he had created it out of hand.

Neither in faith nor in practice was he a Puritan. He saw life as the Puritan had once seen it, with clear and authoritative insight; but he saw it under radically different conditions and with the immense modification of the artistic temperament. Through all manners, customs, dress, institutions, he saw, as the Puritan had seen, the interior reality—the life of the soul. It was as if the externalities of life had no separate existence for him; he was aware only of the immortal element in the show and movement of things. And this immortal element was present in his view, not as a free, expanding energy under normal conditions; but crippled, baffled, beaten about by circumstances; distorted and mis-shapen not only by failure and weakness, but by a deep-going corruption; continually driven back upon itself until it groped blindly in the mysteries of morbid experience. Hawthorne's Puritan inheritance showed itself in his absorption in the problems not only of the spirit, but of the spirit out of harmony with itself and at odds with its own nature.

American fiction began with the application of the most subtle psychology to the study and analysis of character, and Hawthorne, Browne, and Poe are the progenitors of Mr. Henry James and of Mrs. Wharton; with this radical difference, that the earlier writers of fiction did not apply their methods to living tissues; they dealt almost entirely with the past or with phantoms of their own creation. Hawthorne's Puritan inheritance determined the bent of his mind, and gave him the key to a world already fast vanishing below the horizon of thought; but his genius, which was fundamentally artistic and therefore non-Puritan, compelled him to look at the world of the Puritan spiritual tragedy from a distance; and when he fastened on the same aspects of experience in contemporary life, as in " The Blithedale Romance " and " The Marble Faun," he held his figures at arm's length, and never for a moment do we lose consciousness of the fact that we are " moving about in worlds not realized." Inheritance and genius were at odds in Hawthorne; his temperament was sympathetic with his inheritance, and his way of living prepared for and invited the ghostly figures which preoccupied his meditations. But his temperament was also artistic and craved color, vitality, form, beauty; hence the extraordinary firmness and fineness of tissue in his work, its precision of statement and its suggestiveness to the imagination, its beauty born in a feeling not only for the subtle and delicate resources of diction, but for the mystery of relationship between spirit and symbol. Hence, also, the sense of remoteness which is never absent from his work; the feeling that we are looking at his men and women through a veil. In the most poignant moments in "The Scarlet Letter," we are never pierced to the heart as, for instance, in "Anna Karénina," in "Crime and Punishment," in "Poor Folk."

Hawthorne impresses us deeply, but he does not agitate us. When he lays the human soul bare, as he lays bare the soul of Dimmesdale, the process is so deliberate and searching that, when we reach the supreme moment of torture, we seem to have come to it through an intellectual rather than an emotional experience. Even when Hawthorne moves rapidly and with a modicum of analysis to the end of the tale, we seem to be reading, not the annals of our time, but the story of

> . . . old, unhappy, far-off things,
> And battles long ago.

Hawthorne was not only the forerunner of the psychologists in fiction, but he was also the prophet of the symbolists. He does not sacrifice the ethical motive, the searching disclosure of character, to the beauty and suggestiveness of the symbol; but the tales and novels present marvelous symbolic effects and are unfolded with a rich circumstance of symbolism that takes possession of the imagination, and excludes all other objects save those which contribute to the subtle and complete unfolding of the drama. The note-books bear witness on every page to the closeness and exactness of his observation; he saw objects, both natural and human, with perfect clarity of vision. If he lacked Thoreau's inimitable knowledge of the detail of natural life, he had the same sharpness of sight. Nothing escaped him, and nothing was outlined with a careless hand. But the moment a figure appeared in the landscape, the landscape began to relate itself to the figure, to take on its character, to wear the color of its mood, to suggest its innermost experience. As in Poe's tales, familiar things under the clearest sky, in the broadest light, become charged with mystery and meaning, and take possession of the reader's senses while the actors take possession of his imagination. Like Poe, Hawthorne begins by slowly and certainly excluding everything that distracts attention, and gradually closes all avenues of escape until both actors and spectators are isolated in a world remade by the temperament, the passion, the sin which are bearing fruit in the disintegration or reformation of a human soul. The daughter of Rappaccini becomes as deadly as the flowers in her father's garden, and there is not a flower among them which is not exhaling its poison from the minute the spectator sets foot within the fateful place.

The isolation of Hawthorne's life seems, in the light of his work, of a piece with his segregation of the world of his fantasy from the world of reality. The most devoted and chivalrous of lovers to the very end of his life, the most companionable and fascinating of fathers, a loyal friend to the few who possessed his heart and broke through his reserve by sheer force of affection, he was, perhaps, the most detached man of a generation in which men were dominated by the passion for causes, and by zeal for the betterment of their fellows. He had political convictions, and was not only a party man, but an office-holder; but no turn of his party's fortunes ever really touched him, and the absorbing movements of his time awoke no response in his heart. He loved a little group with beautiful tenderness; the rest of mankind he studied. There was a vein of something rich in his imagination, but in his moments of freest expression his style never passed certain limits of reserve, never quite realized the splendor which seemed at times on the very point of spreading the hue of moving passion over his closely packed and subtly phrased sentences. The reticence of his nature was so instinctive, and became so much a part of him, that it held his writing back from that last stage of abandon, of unconscious revelation, which other masters of style reach in their happiest moments. One cannot escape the feeling that the acute New England self-consciousness laid its spell on Hawthorne, as on all the other writers of his section, and that he was never quite free from the haunting fear that he should reveal more than he intended; which is precisely what the greatest writers do, in those brief but glorious hours when they are transported out of and lifted above themselves.

There is not only a touch of pallor on Hawthorne's work, but there is, at times, a suggestion of rusticity in his style; as if he had not quite gained the freedom of his craft. It is here that the provincialism of his early surroundings left its trace; in spite of the rare beauty and distinction of his diction, there appear in it, from time to time, traces of a world of high interests but of narrow artistic associations. The construction of the sentences is, as a rule, not only sound, but full of that kind of felicity which lies within the reach of the man of artistic genius only; but there are also traces of rigidity, the marks of his solitude and detachment and of his isolation from the vital currents of artistic feeling and habit. His style has at times the richness of texture of tapestry or of a rare brocade, but its lines are not always flowing, its folds not always free and perfectly expressive of that which they clothe. Great beauty he certainly has, but radiance was denied him.

One feels in him a curious absence of that element of youth which is the characteristic of all other American writers of his rank except Poe. The gift of youth seems to have been denied both these men of sensitive genius; in a world so new that all fortune seemed within the reach of audacity and energy, there was a touch of Old World tragedy on these children of a young civilization. From neither was the essential pathos of life hidden; neither was diverted or imposed upon by the brave new trappings, the novel and stimulating surroundings, of the old races on the new continent. Both seemed to look through the glamour of immense material possessions to the ancient soul of man, always facing the same fate, always under the shadow of the same failures, calamities, sins; and both sought in art to escape from

HAWTHORNE

the hardness and materialism of an immature civilization.

To Hawthorne, however, was given one re-source which was denied to Poe: the resource of humor. His humor was not contagious like Irving's; it had none of the racy tang of the soil, like Lowell's; it was not quick-footed like Holmes's, in whose work it is continually losing its pervasiveness and gaining the concentration of wit. In Hawthorne, humor takes the form of a gentle brooding over the foibles and weak-nesses of men; often somber, rarely saturnine; gaining a certain effectiveness from its lack of gayety. There is no overflow of buoyant spirits, no flooding of the inlets and recesses of thought and experience with the full, deep movement of a rich, powerful nature, charged with vitality and abounding in health; there is, rather, a quiet, meditative contrast between the externalities and the realities of man's fortunes in this world; the play of a keenly observant, detached, and reflec-tive mind over the surface of life. Hawthorne's humor is full of thought; it never carries him out of himself; it never loses the sense of pro-portion and relation; it is keen, penetrating, searching, full of intelligence. It is so dispassionate and impersonal that it seems at times slightly touched with malice.

The chapter on " The Custom-House," which serves as a preface to " The Scarlet Letter," is an example of the cool, deliberate play of his humor; of its keen and, at times, caustic quality. It is probable that he was not wholly aware of the keenness of his pen, and that the local storm which broke about him when that report of a provincial town appeared was like a bolt out of a clear sky. If his humor shows at times a sharp edge, it does not provoke laughter any more than his pathos brings tears.

His genius was extraordinarily sensitive, but it was not lacking in virility and energy. Isolation brought out the lines of his individuality, and not only compelled him to use the material which was most vitally related to his imagination, and therefore most completely possessed by it, but to create his own methods and form his own style. He shows almost no trace of the influence of other writers; in art, as in life, he stood aloof from his time. The vitality of his genius is shown by the fullness of its expression under such adverse conditions; his distinction is heightened by the fact that it was not gained by free intercourse with the masters of his craft. His art is the more wonderful because he was so entirely self-instructed. He is one of our foremost men of letters by virtue of a distinction which, though self-achieved, is of the finest and highest. He is, all things considered, the most perfect artist in our literature, not only by reason of the temperament, insight, sense of form, and resource of expression which he put into his work, but because his rare and beautiful achievements were made in air so chilling to such aims as his, and in an age in which he was an alien by the very quality of his genius.